IS IT JUST ME OR ARE ALL POLITICIANS SHITE?

IS IT JUST ME OR ARE ALL POLITICIANS SHITE?

THE DUMBEST QUOTES IN THE WORLD, FROM THOSE IN CHARGE OF IT

MARK HANKS AND **BEN GARRETT**

metro

Published by Metro Publishing,
an imprint of John Blake Publishing Ltd,
3 Bramber Court, 2 Bramber Road,
London W14 9PB, England

www.blake.co.uk

First published in hardback in 2006

ISBN-13: 978 184358 164 2
ISBN-10: 1 84358 164 7

British Library Cataloguing-in-Publication Data:

A catalogue record for this book is available from the British Library.

Design by www.envydesign.co.uk

Printed in Great Britain by Creative Print and Design

1 3 5 7 9 10 8 6 4 2

© Text copyright Mark Hanks and Benedict Garrett 2006

Papers used by John Blake Publishing are natural, recyclable
products made from wood grown in sustainable forests. The
manufacturing processes conform to the environmental regulations
of the country of origin.

Every attempt has been made to contact the relevant copyright-
holders, but some were unobtainable. We would be grateful if the
appropriate people could contact us.

CONTENTS

Mark Hanks – for Nicki

Ben Garrett – To my politics teacher,
Mr Alan Palmer. (Five years as a
student of politics and here's the result.
'Proud' just isn't the word!)
And to Charmaine, who will always be
the first lady in my life.

1

STATING THE OBVIOUS

—— STATING THE OBVIOUS ——

'If there is a leadership challenge, it will
take place.'
Lord Baker, Conservative peer

'Outside of the killings, Washington has one of
the lowest crime rates in the country.'
*Marion Barry, former Mayor
of Washington, D.C.*

'The only thing responsible for those terrorist
attacks was terrorism.'
Tony Blair, British Prime Minister

'This party will, ultimately, be judged on its
ability to deliver on its promise'
Tony Blair

'Jesus Christ, Peter, what a misjudgement'
*Tony Blair, to Peter Mandelson as the
truth about his house purchase loan from
Geoffrey Robinson emerged*

———— STATING THE OBVIOUS ————

'We'd like to avoid problems because, when we have problems, we can have troubles.'

> *Wesley Bolin, former Governor of Arizona*

'Suicide is a real threat to health in a modern society.'

> *Virginia Bottomley, former Conservative MP*

'Those who survived the San Francisco earthquake said, "Thank God, I'm still alive." But, of course, those who died, their lives will never be the same again.'

> *Barbara Boxer, US Senator for California*

'Clearly, the future is still to come.'

> *Lord Brooke, Conservative peer,*
> *making a prediction*

'There's no mayor school to attend so I'm figuring it out as I go along. It would have been nice if they'd helped me.'

> *Koleen Brooks, former mayor of*
> *Georgetown, Colorado expelled for*
> *baring her breasts in a local bar*

——— STATING THE OBVIOUS ———

'Foot and mouth is not like flu in animals.'
Nick Brown, Labour MP and former
Agriculture Minister

'This is the worst disaster in California since I was elected.'
Pat Brown, former Governor of California, in
reference to a local flood

'I'm a follower of American politics.'
George W. Bush, US President

'It is clear our nation is reliant upon big foreign oil. More and more of our imports come from overseas.'
George W. Bush

'I was raised in the West. The West of Texas. It's pretty close to California. In more ways than Washington, D.C. is close to California.'
George W. Bush

—— STATING THE OBVIOUS ——

'I think we agree, the past is over.'

George W. Bush

'It's very important for folks to understand that, when there's more trade, there's more commerce.'

George W. Bush

'If you don't stand for anything, you don't stand for anything!'

George W. Bush

'I think war is a dangerous place.'

George W. Bush

'I want to remind you all that, in order to fight and win the war, it requires an expenditure of money that is commiserate with keeping a promise to our troops to make sure that they're well paid, well trained, well equipped.'

George W. Bush

─── STATING THE OBVIOUS ───

'As Luce reminded me, he said, without data, without facts, without information, the discussions about public education mean that a person is just another opinion.'

George W. Bush

'The best way to find these terrorists who hide in holes is to get people coming forth to describe the location of the hole, is to give clues and data.'

George W. Bush

'First, let me make it very clear, poor people aren't necessarily killers. Just because you happen to be not rich doesn't mean you're willing to kill.'

George W. Bush

'When I was young and irresponsible, I was young and irresponsible.'

George W. Bush

'It's important for young men and women who look at the Nebraska champs to understand

———— STATING THE OBVIOUS ————

that quality of life is more than just
blocking shots.'
*George W. Bush, addressing the University of
Nebraska women's volleyball team*

'That's just the nature of democracy. Sometimes
pure politics enters into the rhetoric.'
George W. Bush

'It's clearly a budget. It's got a lot of numbers
in it.'
George W. Bush

'I am mindful not only of preserving executive
powers for myself, but for my predecessors
as well.'
George W. Bush

'If this were a dictatorship, it would be a heck
of a lot easier – so long as I'm the dictator.'
George W. Bush

'It is not Reaganesque to support a tax plan that
is Clinton in nature.'
George W. Bush

—— STATING THE OBVIOUS ——

'I couldn't imagine somebody like Osama bin Laden understanding the joy of Hanukkah.'

George W. Bush

'Ann and I will carry out this equivocal message to the world: Markets must be open.'

George W. Bush

'You teach a child to read, and he or her will be able to pass a literacy test.'

George W. Bush

'The suicide bombings have increased. There's too many of them.'

George W. Bush

'I understand that the unrest in the Middle East creates unrest throughout the region.'

George W. Bush

'It is white.'

George W. Bush, on being asked by a child in Britain what the White House was like.

——— STATING THE OBVIOUS ———

'You have to look at history as an evolution
of society.'

> *Jean Chretien, former Canadian*
> *Prime Minister*

'We'll win the next election because we have a
huge majority over anybody else. We're much
more ahead than anybody else. Never has
there been, after seven years, a government so
way ahead of the opposition.'

> *Jean Chretien*

'The older I get the more passionate I become
about ageism.'

> *Robin Cook, former Labour MP*

'When a great many people are unable to find
work, unemployment results.'
Calvin Coolidge, former US President, discussing
> *the United States economic situation in 1931*

———— STATING THE OBVIOUS ————

'China is a big country, inhabited by
many Chinese.'
> *Charles De Gaulle, former French President*

'America's future is still ahead of us.'
> *Thomas E. Dewey, former Governor of New York*

'Society is not to blame for crime,
criminals are.'
> *Bob Dole, former US Senator and
> Presidential candidate*

'The Internet is a great way to get on the net.'
> *Bob Dole*

'Life is very important to Americans.'
> *Bob Dole*

'The more important things are more important
than the less important.'
> *Stephen Dorrell, Conservative MP*

——— STATING THE OBVIOUS ———

'I strongly support the feeding of children.'
Gerald Ford, 38th US President,
on school dinners

'When I have been asked who caused the riots
and the killing in L.A., my answer has been
direct and simple: Who is to blame for the
riots? The rioters are to blame. Who is to blame
for the killings? The killers are to blame.'
Al Gore, former US Vice-President

'Mars is essentially in the same orbit ... Mars is
somewhat the same distance from the sun,
which is very important. We have seen pictures
where there are canals, we believe, and water.
If there is water that means there is oxygen. If
oxygen, that means we can breathe.'
Al Gore

'I don't think I would use the word greedy, but I
think we went over the top a bit.'
Neil Hamilton, disgraced former Conservative
MP, on the Al Fayed libel case

——— STATING THE OBVIOUS ———

'At least 50 per cent of the population are
women, and the rest men.'

Harriet Harman, Labour MP

'We were unanimous – in fact, everybody
was unanimous.'

Eric Heffer, former Labour MP

'The war situation has developed, not
necessarily to Japan's advantage.'

*Emperor Hirohito, former Emperor of Japan,
announcing surrender in 1945.*

'The future, where most of us are destined to
spend the rest of our lives ...'

*Lord Geoffrey Howe, former Chancellor
of the Exchequer*

'If people had proper locks on their doors,
crime could be prevented before it happens.'

Lord Douglas Hurd, former Home Secretary

——— STATING THE OBVIOUS ———

'It needs to be said that the poor are poor
because they don't have enough money.'
Sir Keith Joseph, former adviser
to Margaret Thatcher

'You cannot roast a wet blanket.'
Mackenzie King, former Canadian Prime Minister

'There are more crimes in Britain now, due to a
huge rise in the crime rate.'
Neil Kinnock, former Labour leader

'British unemployment is rising faster here than
in any other European country.'
Neil Kinnock

'Young people by definition have their future
before them.'
Neil Kinnock

'People who like this sort of thing will find this
the sort of thing they like.'
Abraham Lincoln, 16th US President

——— STATING THE OBVIOUS ———

'Sustainable growth is growth that is sustainable.'

John Major, former British Conservative Prime Minister

'The world has gone through a tremendous change recently, both nationally and internationally.'

John Major

'A soundbite never buttered a parsnip.'

John Major

'For the first time in 50 years, bus passenger numbers have risen to their highest level ever.'

John Prescott, Deputy Prime Minister

'For NASA, space is still a high priority.'

Dan Quayle, former US Vice-President

'Quite frankly, teachers are the only profession that teach our children.'

Dan Quayle

———— STATING THE OBVIOUS————

'Hawaii has always been a very pivotal role in the Pacific. It is IN the Pacific. It is a part of the United States that is an island that is right here.'

Dan Quayle

'If we don't succeed we run the risk of failure.'

Dan Quayle

'This election is about who's going to be the next President of the United States!'

Dan Quayle

'We're going to have the best-educated American people in the world.'

Dan Quayle

'Abortion is advocated only by persons who have themselves been born.'

Ronald Reagan, 40th US President

——— STATING THE OBVIOUS ———

'Well, I learned a lot … I went down to Latin America to find out from them and learn their views. You'd be surprised. They're all individual countries.'

Ronald Reagan

'I believe in heredity. It is something we all have.'

Lord Rees-Mogg, cross-bench life peer

'The streets are safe in Philadelphia – it's only the people who make them unsafe.'

Frank Rizzo, ex-police chief and Mayor of Philadelphia

'We do know of certain knowledge that he [Osama Bin Laden] is either in Afghanistan, or in some other country, or dead.'

Donald Rumsfeld, US Defence Secretary

'Headmasters of schools tend to be men.'

Clare Short, Labour MP and former Cabinet Minister

——— STATING THE OBVIOUS ———

'The biggest challenge of the new decade is to
encourage people to work longer.'

Andrew Smith, Labour MP

'Our Cabinet is always unanimous – except
when we disagree.'

*William Vander Zalm, former
Premier of British Columbia*

'Pensioners were not born yesterday.'

*Steven Webb, Liberal Democrat MP
and Health spokesman*

'Prison is and never has been a soft option.'

Ann Widdecombe, Conservative MP

❷

MISCELLANEOUS STUPIDITY

—— MISCELLANEOUS STUPIDITY ——

'The single, overwhelming two facts are...'
Paddy Ashdown, former Liberal
Democrats leader

'I'd like the taxes to go to those parents lucky enough to have children.'
Tony Banks, former Labour MP

'Tourists go home with the photographs showing them with one foot in the northern hemisphere and one in the southern.'
Rosie Barnes, former SDP MP,
on Greenwich

'What right does Congress have to go around making laws just because they deem it necessary?'
Marion Barry, former Mayor
of Washington, D.C.

'Mussolini never killed anyone. Mussolini used to send people on vacation in internal exile.'
Silvio Berlusconi, former Italian Prime Minister

—— MISCELLANEOUS STUPIDITY——

'Eighty-five per cent of the Italian press is left-wing and among the judges it is even worse ... There is a cancer in Italy that we have to treat: the politicisation of the magistracy.'

Silvio Berlusconi

'I don't make predictions. I never have and I never will.'

Tony Blair, British Prime Minister

'If we want to stop the defence industry operating in this country, we can do so. The result incidentally would be that someone else supplies the arms that we supply.'

Tony Blair

"Mine is the first generation able to contemplate the possibility that we may live our entire lives without going to war or sending our children to war."

Tony Blair

—— MISCELLANEOUS STUPIDITY——

'Bringing up children on your own is very difficult even where there are two parents.'
Virginia Bottomley, former Conservative MP

'If crime went down 100 per cent, it would still be 50 times higher than it should be.'
John Bowman, councilman, on the high crime rate in Washington, D.C.

'If the terriers and bariffs are torn down, this economy will grow.'
George W. Bush, US President

'I'm so pleased to be able to say hello to Bill Scranton. He's one of the great Pennsylvania political families.'
George W. Bush

'I am a person who recognises the fallacy of humans.'
George W. Bush

—— MISCELLANEOUS STUPIDITY——

'I recently met with the finance minister of the Palestinian Authority, was very impressed by his grasp of finances.'

George W. Bush

'This very week in 1989, there were protests in East Berlin and in Leipzig. By the end of that year, every communist dictatorship in Central America had collapsed.'

George W. Bush

'Iran would be dangerous if they have a nuclear weapon.'

George W. Bush

'Now, there are some who would like to rewrite history – revisionist historians is what I like to call them.'

George W. Bush

'I want to thank the astronauts who are with us, the courageous special entrepreneurs who set such a wonderful example for the young of our country.'

George W. Bush

—— MISCELLANEOUS STUPIDITY ——

'I want it to be said that the Bush administration was a results-oriented administration, because I believe the results of focusing our attention and energy on teaching children to read and having an education system that's responsive to the child and to the parents, as opposed to mired in a system that refuses to change, will make America what we want it to be – a more literate country and a hopefuller country.'

George W. Bush

'See, free nations are peaceful nations. Free nations don't attack each other. Free nations don't develop weapons of mass destruction.'

George W. Bush

'We need an energy bill that encourages consumption.'

George W. Bush

'We ended the rule of one of history's worst tyrants and, in so doing, we not only freed the American people, we made our own people more secure.'

George W. Bush

—— MISCELLANEOUS STUPIDITY——

'The problem with the French is that they don't have a word for entrepreneur.'

George W. Bush, practising his French

'I love the idea of a school in which people come to get educated and stay in the state in which they're educated.'

George W. Bush

'Do you have blacks, too?'

George W. Bush, to Brazilian President Fernando Cardoso

'You see, the Senate wants to take away some of the powers of the administrative branch.'

George W. Bush

'This administration is doing everything we can to end the stalemate in an efficient way. We're making the right decisions to bring the solution to an end.'

George W. Bush

——MISCELLANEOUS STUPIDITY——

'Natural gas is hemispheric. I like to call it
hemispheric in nature because it is a product
that we can find in our neighbourhoods.'

George W. Bush

'So thank you for reminding me about the
importance of being a good mom and a great
volunteer as well.'

George W. Bush

'I am mindful of the difference between the
executive branch and the legislative branch. I
assured all four of these leaders that I know
the difference, and that difference is they pass
the laws and I execute them.'

George W. Bush

'The legislature's job is to write law. It's the
executive branch's job to interpret law.'

George W. Bush

——MISCELLANEOUS STUPIDITY——

'The public education system in America is one of the most important foundations of our democracy. After all, it is where children from all over America learn to be responsible citizens, and learn to have the skills necessary to take advantage of our fantastic opportunistic society.'

George W. Bush

'The Iraqis need to be very much involved. They were the people that was brutalised by this man.'

George W. Bush, on stabilising Iraq

'I've got very good relations with President Mubarak and Crown Prince Abdallah and the King of Jordan, Gulf Coast countries.'

George W. Bush

'A lot of times in the rhetoric, people forget the facts. And the facts are that thousands of small businesses – Hispanically owned or otherwise – pay taxes at the highest marginal rate.'

George W. Bush, speaking to the Hispanic Chamber of Commerce

—— MISCELLANEOUS STUPIDITY ——

'They misunderestimated me.'

George W. Bush

'I've coined new words, like, misunderstanding and Hispanically.'

George W. Bush, failing to refer to a previous blunder

'Rarely is the question asked: Is our children learning?'

George W. Bush

'We cannot let terrorists and rogue nations hold this nation hostile or hold our allies hostile.'

George W. Bush

'We hold dear what our Declaration of Independence says, that all have got uninalienable rights, endowed by a Creator.'

George W. Bush, trying to be un-unintelligent

—— MISCELLANEOUS STUPIDITY——

'Unfairly but truthfully, our party has been tagged as being against things. Anti-immigrant, for example. And we're not a party of anti-immigrants. Quite the opposite. We're a party that welcomes people.'

George W. Bush, honestly speaking

'Reading is the basics for all learning.'

George W. Bush, announcing his 'Reading First' initiative

'Well, I think, if you say you're going to do something and don't do it, that's trustworthiness.'

George W. Bush

'My trip to Asia begins here in Japan for an important reason. It begins here because for a century and a half now, America and Japan have formed one of the great and enduring alliances of modern times. From that alliance has come an era of peace in the Pacific.'

George W. Bush, slightly forgetful

——MISCELLANEOUS STUPIDITY——

'I understand small business growth. I was one.'
George W. Bush

'The folks who conducted to act on our country on September 11th made a big mistake. They underestimated America. They underestimated our resolve, our determination, our love for freedom. They misunderestimated the fact that we love a neighbour in need. They misunderestimated the compassion of our country. I think they misunderestimated the will and determination of the Commander-in-Chief, too.'
George W. Bush

'I think anybody who doesn't think I'm smart enough to handle the job is underestimating.'
George W. Bush

'Dick Cheney and I do not want this nation to be in a recession. We want anybody who can find work to be able to find work.'
George W. Bush

—— MISCELLANEOUS STUPIDITY——

'Laura and I really don't realize how bright our children is sometimes until we get an objective analysis.'

George W. Bush

'We've tripled the amount of money – I believe it's from $50 million up to $195 million available.'

George W. Bush crunches some numbers

'I know how hard it is for you to put food on your family.'

George W. Bush

'Can't living with the bill means it won't become law.'

George W. Bush, who is teetotal.

'Our priorities is our faith.'

George W. Bush

'Families is where our nation finds hope, where wings take dream.'

George W. Bush

—— MISCELLANEOUS STUPIDITY ——

'Will the highways on the Internet become more few?'

>   *George W. Bush, asking a tough question*

'They want the federal government controlling Social Security like it's some kind of federal programme.'

>   *George W. Bush*

'Laura and I are proud to call John and Michelle Engler our friends. I know you're proud to call him governor. What a good man the Englers are.'

>   *George W. Bush*

'The most important job is not to be governor, or first lady in my case.'

>   *George W. Bush, on his*
>   *identity crisis*

'Put the "off" button on.'

>   *George W. Bush, advising parents worried by*
>   *graphic content on television*

—— MISCELLANEOUS STUPIDITY——

'Its one of the great urban myths that people get pregnant in order to have children.'

Menzies Campbell, Leader of the Liberal Democrats

'My contacts have told me where Saddam Hussein is hiding. He is in Saudi Arabia.'

Naomi Campbell, model

'Seals don't eat beef. I was interviewed one day in France. I explained one of the problems is we have too many seals. A reporter came to me and asked if it is true that seals eat cod. I don't know. I'm not a seal. But I can tell you seals don't eat beef because the seals are not living in Alberta.'

Jean Chretien, former Canadian Prime Minister

'And Canada was next. In 1863, we became the third federation in the world.'

Jean Chretien, teaching a school class about Canada, which became a federation in 1867

—— MISCELLANEOUS STUPIDITY ——

'They've managed to keep their unemployment low although their overall unemployment is high.'

Bill Clinton, 42nd US President

'I'm not going to have some reporters pawing through our papers. We are the President.'

Hillary Clinton, wife of Bill

'My vision is to make the most diverse state on earth, and we have people from every planet on the earth in this state. We have the sons and daughters of every, of people from every planet, of every country on earth.'

Gray Davis, former Governor of California

'Not a single person has asked me about the selection process – only journalists.'

Gerald Ford, 38th US President

'That is what has made America last these past 200 centuries.'

Gerald Ford

—— MISCELLANEOUS STUPIDITY——

'President Carter speaks loudly and carries a fly spotter, a fly swasher – it's been a long day.'
Gerald Ford

'I love sports. Whenever I can, I always watch the Detroit Tigers on the radio.'
Gerald Ford

'We're sending 23 million leaflets to every household in Britain.'
Norman Fowler, former Conservative MP

"Saddam Hussein greeted me with a handshake, which, again to my surprise, is surprisingly soft considering how many people that hand had dispatched, allegedly. I think he's quite a forbidding presence, too forbidding a presence to be charming. But he's interesting."
George Galloway, former Labour MP and leader of Respect

'Its not the future I'm talking about, I'm talking about tomorrow …'
John Gummer, Conservative MP

——MISCELLANEOUS STUPIDITY——

'The best cure for insomnia is to get a lot of sleep.'

S.I. Hayakawa, US Senator

'You can't just let nature run wild.'

Wally Hickel, former Governor of Alaska

'I do not believe that one person's poverty is caused by another's wealth.'

Michael Howard, former Conservative leader

'We've got to pause and ask ourselves: How much clean air do we need?'

Lee Iacocca, US industrialist

'How on earth do the birds know it is a sanctuary?'

Sir Keith Joseph, former Conservative MP, on visiting a bird sanctuary

'Both economically, politically and socially ...'

Neil Kinnock, former Labour leader

—— MISCELLANEOUS STUPIDITY——

'I was stunned with outrage.'

Neil Kinnock

'My seven year old, who is now ten ...'

Lady Olga Maitland, former
Conservative MP

'The IRA have been isolated in the eyes of the world and many other people.'

John Major, former British
Conservative Prime Minister

'There is always a choice of whether one does it last week, this week, or next week.'

John Major

'"If" is a very big preposition.'

John Major

'We are not wholly an island, except geographically.'

John Major

—— MISCELLANEOUS STUPIDITY ——

'I will turn directly to the Asylum Bill later.'

John Major

'When the President does it, that means that it's not illegal.'

Richard Nixon, 37th US President

'To break the two-party monopoly will be very difficult.'

David Owen, former Labour and SDP MP

'The Unionist Parliament was without a spine or backbone.'

Ian Paisley, Northern Irish Politician

'Who is King Billy? Go home, man, and read your bible.'

Ian Paisley, referring to William of Orange

'Saint Patrick was a Protestant.'

Ian Paisley

—— MISCELLANEOUS STUPIDITY——

'I believe that all illegal organisations should be outlawed.'

Ian Paisley

'I believe that God created man. I object to teachers saying that we came from monkeys.'

Ian Paisley, speaking in 1980

'Our record bears out that we seek no territory, we seek no dominance, we seek friends.'

Colin Powell, US Secretary of State

'It's great to be back on terra cotta.'

John Prescott, Deputy Prime Minister

'Now, give over, John, even the prime minister has done a lot more to do.'

John Prescott

"People like Greenpeace should look at the ruddy facts instead of looking for stunts,"

John Prescott, speaking after activists climbed on to his roof and installed solar panels in a protest at the Government's energy policy.

—— MISCELLANEOUS STUPIDITY ——

'Poverty isn't about money. It's a whole way of life.'

> *John Profumo, former Conservative MP*

'The trend toward democracy is inevitable: but it can be stopped.'

> *Dan Quayle, former US Vice-President*

'May our nation continue to be the beakon of hope to the world.'

> *Dan Quayle, in the Quayles'*
> *1989 Christmas card*

'It is time for the human race to join the solar system.'

> *Dan Quayle*

'I was recently on a tour of Latin America, and the only regret I have was that I didn't study Latin harder in school so I could converse with those people.'

> *Dan Quayle*

—— MISCELLANEOUS STUPIDITY——

'One word sums up probably the responsibility of any Vice-President, and that one word is "to be prepared".'

Dan Quayle

'We have a firm commitment to NATO, we are a part of NATO. We have a firm commitment to Europe. We are a part of Europe.'

Dan Quayle, on the United States

'There are lots more people in the House. I don't know exactly – I've never counted, but at least a couple hundred.'

Dan Quayle, on the difference between the House and Senate

'We are not ready for an unforeseen event that may or may not occur.'

Dan Quayle. Presumably this speech was unprepared.

——MISCELLANEOUS STUPIDITY——

'Hawaii is a unique state. It is a small state. It is a state that is by itself. It is a ... it is different from the other 49 states. Well, all states are different, but it's got a particularly unique situation.'

Dan Quayle

'Potatoe.'

Dan Quayle, correcting a schoolchild's spelling of 'potato'

'The global importance of the Middle East is that it keeps the Near East and the Far East from encroaching on each other.'

Dan Quayle

'I have made good judgements in the past. I have made good judgements in the future.'

Dan Quayle

'My fellow astronauts ...'

Dan Quayle, forgetting his job

—— MISCELLANEOUS STUPIDITY——

'This fellow they've nominated claims he's the new Thomas Jefferson. Well, let me tell you something; I knew Thomas Jefferson. He was a friend of mine and, Governor, you're no Thomas Jefferson!'

Ronald Reagan, 40th US President referring to the third US President, Thomas Jefferson, who died in 1826

'Eighty per cent of air pollution comes not from chimneys and auto exhaust pipes, but from plants and trees.'

Ronald Reagan

'We're not building missiles to fight a war. We're building missiles to preserve the peace.'

Ronald Reagan

'Trees cause more pollution than automobiles do.'

Ronald Reagan

'Fascism was really the basis for the New Deal.'

Ronald Reagan

——MISCELLANEOUS STUPIDITY——

'We think there is a parallel between federal involvement in education and the decline in profit over recent years.'

Ronald Reagan

'As Henry VIII said to each of his three wives, "I won't keep you long."'

Ronald Reagan. Henry VIII had,
of course, six wives.

'If you won't tell me who told you that, it's not worth the paper it was written on.'

Sir Malcolm Rifkind, former Parliamentary
Spokesman for the Conservatives

'A man could not be in two places at the same time unless he were a bird.'

Boyle Roche, 18th-century Member
of Parliament from Tralee

'I answer in the affirmative with an emphatic – "No".'

Boyle Roche

—— MISCELLANEOUS STUPIDITY——

'Half the lies our opponents tell about us are not true.'

> *Boyle Roche*

'Our nuclear power stations are as safe as they can possibly be, and are getting safer all the time.'

> *Hugh Rossi, former Conservative MP*

'In Poland, or some other South American country...'

> *Arthur Scargill, former President of the*
> *National Union of Mineworkers*

'I think that gay marriage should be between a man and a woman.'

> *Arnold Schwarzenegger, actor*
> *and Governor of California*

'That was another thing I will never forgive the Republican Party for. I was ashamed to call myself a Republican during that period.'

> *Arnold Schwarzenegger, on the*
> *Clinton impeachment*

—— MISCELLANEOUS STUPIDITY ——

'Is the West Bank a publicly or privately owned institution?'

Enzo Scotti, former Italian Minister
for the Interior

'The trend in the rise in unemployment is downward.'

Gillian Shephard, former Conservative MP

'I do not know what detox is. But whatever it is, I am not doing it.'

Nicholas Soames, Conservative MP

'To listen to some people in politics, you'd think "nice" was a four-letter word.'

Lord Steel, Liberal Democrat peer

'In America any boy may become President and I suppose it's just one of the risks he takes.'

Adlai Stevenson, former US
Representative to the United Nations

—— MISCELLANEOUS STUPIDITY——

'We said zero, and I think any statistician will tell you that when you're dealing with very big numbers, zero must mean plus or minus a few.'
Lord Waldegrave, Conservative peer

'Anyone would think we were living on some island somewhere.'
George Walden, Conservative MP

'I've read about foreign policy and studied, I now know the number of continents.'
George Wallace, 1968 Presidential candidate

'I have always said it is a great mistake ever to pre-judge the past.'
William Whitelaw, former Conservative MP and Secretary of State for Northern Ireland

'I believe absolutely that the world was created in seven phases and science has never disputed the order of creation.'
Ann Widdecombe, MP

——MISCELLANEOUS STUPIDITY——

'I can tell you exactly how many trade union members voted for the SDP – about 20 per cent.'
Shirley Williams, former Labour and SDP MP, now Liberal Democrat leader in the Lords

❸
(Dis) FIGURES
OF SPEECH

—— (Dis) FIGURES OF SPEECH ——

'The IRA will stick to their guns on
decommissioning.'

Gerry Adams, President of Sinn Fein

'Bridge-building is a one-way street.'

Jonathan Aitken, disgraced
former Conservative MP

'Nothing happened until I pressed the minister
on the floor of the House.'

Lord Alton, cross-bench peer

'That's a fascinating crystal ball, but I'll tell you
the other side of the coin.'

Jeffrey Archer, disgraced Conservative peer

'If Europe stays still, it will start going
backwards.'

Paddy Ashdown, former Liberal Democrat leader

'Mrs Thatcher's silence has resounded like
thunder across Britain.'

Paddy Ashdown

—— (Dis) FIGURES OF SPEECH ——

'Norman Lamont knows his political future is behind him.'

Tony Banks, former Labour MP,
referring to the former Chancellor

'Bringing the leadership to its knees occasionally is a good way of keeping it on its toes.'

Tony Banks

'If you let that sort of thing go on, your bread and butter will be cut right from under your feet.'

Ernest Bevin, British trade
unionist and statesman

'Now is not the time for soundbites. I can feel the hand of history on my shoulder.'

Tony Blair, British Prime Minister, on the signing
of the Good Friday Agreement

'The BBC must blow their own trumpet and have others blow their own trumpet for them.'

Paul Boateng, former Labour MP

—— (Dis) FIGURES OF SPEECH ——

'That particular honeymoon has completely burst.'
> *Virginia Bottomley, former Conservative MP*

'The Militants in Liverpool spend money like water, as if it came from outer space.'
> *Sir Rhodes Boyson, former Conservative MP*

'These cornerstones were the centre of the Chancellor's policy.'
> *Gordon Brown, Chancellor of the Exchequer*

'There's no question that, the minute I got elected, the storm clouds on the horizon were getting nearly directly overhead.'
> *George W. Bush, US President*

'I firmly believe the death tax is good for people from all walks of life all throughout our society.'
> *George W. Bush*

'We ought to make the pie higher.'
> *George W. Bush*

—— (Dis) FIGURES OF SPEECH ——

'Security is the essential roadblock to
achieving the road map to peace.'

George W. Bush

'The senator has got to understand if he's
going to have – he can't have it both ways.
He can't take the high horse and then
claim the low road.'

George W. Bush

'I have said that the sanction regime is like
Swiss cheese – that meant that they weren't
very effective.'

George W. Bush

'I think there is a Trojan horse lurking in the
weeds trying to pull a fast one on the
Americans.'

George W. Bush, live on the radio

'It's no use trying to pin a donkey on a few
individuals, however much Lord Justice Scott
wants to.'

Alan Clark, former Conservative MP

—— (Dis) FIGURES OF SPEECH ——

'We can beat the Liberals even with one engine
tied behind our backs.'
> *Joe Clark, former Canadian Prime Minister*

'The Americans have sowed the seed, and now
they have reaped the whirlwind.'
Sebastian Coe, athlete and former Conservative MP

'That wasn't the only thing he did. That was just
the froth on the cake.'
> *Julian Critchley, former Conservative MP*

'Businessmen should stand or fall on their
own two feet.'
> *Edwina Currie, writer, broadcaster and*
> *former Conservative Politician*

'There's no smoke without mud being flung
around.'   *Edwina Currie*

'If Lincoln was alive today, he'd roll over in his
grave.'
Gerald Ford, 38th US President, of Abraham Lincoln

—— (Dis) FIGURES OF SPEECH ——

'It is no use for the honourable Member to shake his head in the teeth of his own words.'

> *William Gladstone, 19th-century*
> *British Prime Minister*

'A zebra does not change its spots.'

> *Al Gore, former US Vice-President*

'A leopard never changes his stripes.'

> *Al Gore*

'The NUPE candidate should put her voice where her mouth is.'

> *Derek Hatton, chat radio host,*
> *businessman and style guru*

'I went up the greasy pole of politics step by step.'

> *Michael Heseltine, former Conservative MP*

'It's not something you can do like a fairy godmother from the top of the Christmas tree.'

> *Michael Heseltine*

—— (Dis) FIGURES OF SPEECH ——

'The Government are shrugging their feet
over this issue.'

Doug Hoyle, former Labour MP

'The IRA are deadly serious about a cessation
of violence.'

John Hume, former Northern Ireland MP

'Paddy Ashdown was dealt a difficult pack of
cards – but he kept his eye on the ball all the
way through.'

Charles Kennedy, former Liberal Democrat leader

'This is a window of opportunity for us to
step into.'

Tom King, former Conservative MP

'It is a hothouse in a goldfish bowl.'

Neil Kinnock, former Labour leader

'They pushed their nomination down my throat
behind my neck.'

*Ramsay MacDonald, former British
Labour Prime Minister*

—— (Dis) FIGURES OF SPEECH ——

'One doesn't know how many potatoes will appear over the horizon.'

David Madel, former Conservative MP

'When your back is against the wall, the only thing to do is turn around and fight.'

John Major, former British Conservative
Prime Minister

'United Nations' goodwill may be a bottomless pit, but it's by no mean limitless.'

John Major

'This is the first step in a chain that will unfold.'

David Mellor, former Conservative MP
turned radio pundit

'The door is now open. What we have to do is push it fully ajar.'

Elliot Morley, Environment Minister

—— (Dis) FIGURES OF SPEECH ——

'You can argue about that until the cows
come home.'

> *Elliot Morley, in a debate about animal
> slaughter during the foot-and-mouth crisis*

'At the end of the day, isn't it time we called
it a day?'

> *John Morris, former Labour MP*

'We are not going to stand idly by and be
murdered in our beds.'

> *Ian Paisley, Northern Ireland politician*

'We thank you from the deepest bowls of our
heart.'

> *Anne Picking, Westminster PPC for East Lothian*

'We are unpacking the damage they have done.'

> *John Prescott, Deputy Prime Minister*

'Here we have a government disintegrating
between our eyes.'

> *John Prescott, referring to the
> Major Government*

—— (Dis) FIGURES OF SPEECH ——

'I want to be Robin to Bush's Batman.'
Dan Quayle, former US Vice-President

'This isn't a man who is leaving with his head between his legs.'
Dan Quayle

'The cup of our trouble is running over, but, alas, is not yet full.'
Boyle Roche, 18th-century Member of Parliament from Tralee

'Along the untrodden paths of the future, I can see the footprints of an unseen hand.'
Boyle Roche

'If anyone thinks I'm there to throw water on a fire, they're wrong.'
Donald Rumsfeld, US Defence Secretary, who made a surprise visit to Baghdad

—— (Dis) FIGURES OF SPEECH ——

'We blocked them inside the city. Their rear
is blocked.'
> *Mohammed Saeed al-Sahaf, former Iraqi*
> *Information Minister, on the allied forces*

'That's the way the cookie bounces.'
> *Vic Shiro, former Mayor of New Orleans*

'Clearly the Prime Minister's devious hand
is afoot.'
> *John Smith, former Labour leader*

'This is John Major's last desperate throw of the
dice and we will ensure it scores a double blank.'
> *Jack Straw, Labour MP*

'Labour are pushing lies through our doorstep.'
> *Lord Waldegrave, Conservative peer*

'I have a thermometer in my mouth and I am
listening to it all the time.'
> *William Whitelaw, former conservative MP*
> *and Secretary of State for Northern Ireland*

4

INSULTS AND PUTDOWNS

—— INSULTS AND PUTDOWNS ——

'Allowing women to mix with men is the root of every evil and catastrophe.'
Abdulaziz bin Abdullah al-Sheikh, Saudi Arabia's most senior Muslim cleric

'Every other friend of his has been given something or other. I have been offered absolutely nothing. God knows what I did to offend him.'
Clive Anderson, barrister and broadcaster, on Tony Blair, whom he knew as a lawyer

'Gordon Brown? He's vacuous, ridiculous, utterly pathetic.'
Tony Benn

"If Glenn Hoddle is right then I must have been a failed football manager in a previous existence."
[Hoddle had commented on a link between disability and sins in a past life] David Blunkett

—— INSULTS AND PUTDOWNS ——

'Here's 20p – phone all of them.'
Gordon Brown, Chancellor of the Exchequer, responding to Peter Mandelson when Mandelson wanted to borrow 10p to phone a friend

"There is nothing that you could say to me now that I could ever believe."
[To Tony Blair] Gordon Brown

"You're an analogue politician in a digital age."
David Cameron, Leader of the Conservative Party, to Gordon Brown

'UKIP is a bunch of fruit cakes and loonies and closet racists mostly.'
David Cameron, makes clear the difference between the UK Independence Party and the Tories

"In a carbon conscious world, we got a fossil fuel chancellor."
David Cameron, to Gordon Brown

—— INSULTS AND PUTDOWNS ——

"It seems to me they are joined at the hip, Mr Brown and Mr Blair. That's a demonstration, it seems to me, that neither of them is willing to let the other out of their sight,"

Sir Menzies Campbell, , on Gordon Brown and Tony Blair appearing next to each other again to launch their manifesto

'Stanley Baldwin was an epileptic corpse.'

Winston Churchill, former British Prime Minister

'Ming is an old Tory. He is someone Conservatives can do business with.'

Kenneth Clarke, former Tory Chancellor, subtly jibes at Liberal Democrat leader Menzies Campbell

'I do not think we impress the public if we set too low a value on our own worth.'

Robin Cook, former Foreign Secretary and Leader of the House of Commons, on MPs and their pay increase

—— INSULTS AND PUTDOWNS ——

"The trouble is that when Mr Howard talks about immigration he just doesn't sound nice."
Robin Cook

'Frankly, sharing a media market with Chuck Schumer is like sharing a banana with a monkey. Take a little bite of it, and he will throw his own faeces at you.'
*Jon Corzine, on New Jersey Senator,
on New York Senator Charles Schumer's
fondness for publicity*

'What has she ever done apart from abolish cellulite. Does that deserve admiration?'
*Edwina Currie, writer, broadcaster and former
Conservative Politician, on Liz Hurley*

'I'm hoping that now the poison has been drained, we can all sit back and learn lessons from it.'
*Paul Dacre, Editor of the Daily Mail, on
Alastair Campbell, former Labour spin doctor*

—— INSULTS AND PUTDOWNS ——

'The difference between a misfortune and a calamity is this: If Gladstone fell into the Thames, it would be a misfortune. But if someone dragged him out again, that would be a calamity.'

Benjamin Disraeli, 19th-century British Prime Minister

'There they are. See no evil, hear no evil, and ... evil.'

Bob Dole, former US Senator and Presidential candidate, watching former US Presidents Carter, Ford and Nixon standing by each other at a White House event

'You are a silly, rude bitch and, since you are a potential breeder, God help the next generation.'

Sir Nicholas Fairbairn, former Conservative MP, to a female heckler

'Getting a pet might be a way of humanising yourself, but a Labrador won't fool me.'

Ken Follett, author, on Peter Mandelson

—— INSULTS AND PUTDOWNS ——

"He turned out to be our first karaoke Prime Minister - always desperate to perform and saying whatever people want to hear,"
> *Liam Fox, at the launch of a cinema advert showing Tony Blair smiling.*

'A small man intoxicated by being allowed to run around with the big aggressive powerful boys after so many years as a corduroy-clad peacenik.'
> *George Galloway, former Labour MP and leader of Respect, on then Foreign Secretary Robin Cook*

"I have met Saddam Hussein exactly the same number of times as Donald Rumsfeld met him. The difference is that Donald Rumsfeld met him to sell him guns and to give him maps the better to target those guns."
> *George Galloway*

'These poor old ducks seek refuge in them because they cannot cope with modern women.'
> *Teresa Gorman, former Conservative MP, after the Carlton Club denied women full membership*

—— INSULTS AND PUTDOWNS ——

'Robin is running a "stop Peter" campaign,
Peter is running a "stop Gordon" campaign
and John Prescott always seems to be running
a "stop John Prescott" campaign.'
William Hague, former Conservative leader

'Wennlund has an obscure, undistinguished
record, and he's a poor dresser, too.'
Ray Hanania, candidate for Illinois state
representative, referring to incumbent
Larry Wennlund

'Anyone curious about the nature of life on
Death Row should consult Mr Iain Duncan
Smith. He is there now.'
Sir Max Hastings, journalist

'If there were a Speech Crimes Tribunal set up
in The Hague, John Prescott would be in the
dock for committing syntactical genocide.'
Jerry Hayes, former Conservative MP

—— INSULTS AND PUTDOWNS ——

'Margaret Thatcher adds the diplomacy of Alf Garnett to the economics of Arthur Daley.'
Lord Healey, Labour peer

"This grammar school boy is not going to take any lessons from a public school boy on children from less privileged backgrounds."
Michael Howard, former Conservative Leader

"So far this year they have compared me to Fagin, to Shylock and to a flying pig. This morning Peter Hain even called me a mongrel."
Michael Howard

'You cannot behave as a lager lout and remain as Deputy Prime Minister.'
Michael Heseltine, Conservative MP, on John Prescott

'If the word "No" was removed from the English language, Ian Paisley would be speechless.'
John Hume, former Northern Ireland MP

—— INSULTS AND PUTDOWNS ——

'Tony Blair is just Bill Clinton's toyboy.'
Saddam Hussein, former President of Iraq

'It was a bitter irony that our first woman
Prime Minister was Thatcher: a case of a man
in a frock.'
Glenda Jackson, Labour MP

'What the whole Iraq episode explodes so
far is the idea that Blair is a nice man with
a vacuous grin and no strong convictions.'
*Lord Jenkins, former Labour
and SDP MP*

'I have had more women by accident than JFK
had on purpose.'
Lyndon B. Johnson, 36th US President

'The problem with Lloyd Webber's music in not
that it sounds as if it were by other composers,
but that it sounds as if it were written by Lloyd
Webber.'
Gerald Kaufman, Labour MP

—— INSULTS AND PUTDOWNS ——

'Words cannot express my regret at the news that Anthony Wedgewood Benn has decided to retire from Parliament. My regret is that he has left it 20 years too late.'

Gerald Kaufman

"I don't think Tony Blair would be a very plausible used car salesman."

Charles Kennedy, former leader of the Liberal Democrats, when pressed by reporters as to whether he would trust Mr Blair.

'I want to start by saying something nice about President Bush. Of all the presidents we've had with the last name of Bush, his economic plan ranks in the top two.'

John Kerry, Democrat Senator

"What makes me sick is that when I come across someone who is guilty of genocide I do not get on a plane and go to Baghdad and grovel at his feet"

Oona King, former Labour MP for Bethnal Green and Bow refers to George Galloway, who won the seat from her

—— INSULTS AND PUTDOWNS ——

'Nixon has been sitting in the White House while George McGovern has been exposing himself to the people of the United States.'
Frank Licht, former Governor of Rhode Island, on the campaign trail for McGovern in 1972

'It would be quite nice if the American ambassador in Britain could pay the charge that everybody else is paying and not try and [evade] it like some chiselling little crook.'
Ken Livingstone, Mayor of London

'Robin Cook is the only foreign Secretary in 700 years who has more trouble at home than he has abroad. But don't mock. One day his looks will go.'
John Major, former British Conservative Prime Minister

—— INSULTS AND PUTDOWNS ——

"To see young political leaders of the developed world act in ways that undermine some of the noblest attempts of humanity to deal with historical legacies, pains me greatly and makes me worry immensely about our future.'

Nelson Mandela, former President of ANC and South Africa, in London, having a go at George Bush and Tony Blair

'What I think about Mr Blunkett is almost unprintable. Illiberal, yes, is the term that would spring to mind, but this is a man playing to a certain gallery, and the gallery he feels he has to play to is the law-and-order gallery.'

Michael Mansfield, QC

'I keep a video of Tony Blair reading Corinthians at Diana's funeral and threaten to show it to anyone who is impressed by the PM's sincerity.'

Bob Marshall-Andrews, Labour MP

—— INSULTS AND PUTDOWNS ——

'Even though most gay men and women blame her for Section 28, they still admire her as a drag idol.'

Ivan Massow, former chairman of the Institute of Contemporary Arts, on Margaret Thatcher

'David Lloyd-George is a goat-footed bard, a half-human visitor to our age from the hag-ridden magic and enchanted woods of Celtic antiquity.'

John Maynard Keynes, economist

'He's a patronising bastard. I mean he is ... I mean he really is.'

Henry McLeish, former Scottish MP, discussing Labour MP John Reid with Helen Liddell after the Westminster Election. The comment was accidentally recorded by a radio reporter

'When I first arrived in 1997, John Prescott thought that biodiversity was a kind of washing powder.'

Michael Meacher, Labour MP and former Environment Minister

—— INSULTS AND PUTDOWNS ——

"New Labour did not invent lying, but they
have raised it to the status of high art,"
David Mellor, former Tory Cabinet Minister

'President Bush ... is really a giant corporation
in the White House masquerading as a human
being.'
Ralph Nader, US Presidential candidate in 2004

'Michael Foot is a kind of walking obituary for
the Labour Party.'
*Chris Patten, last British Governor of Hong Kong,
on the former leader of the Labour Party*

'If you don't get out of this shot, I'll stick one on
your chin.'
*John Prescott, Deputy Prime Minister,
after being complimented on his tie while
being interviewed for television*

'I mean, IDS – cor blimey, he's the man – what did
he say? – "unite or die"? – I think it's more likely
to be "Die Another Day" the way he's going.'
John Prescott, on Iain Duncan Smith

—— INSULTS AND PUTDOWNS ——

'He's been taught new hand gestures for when he is speaking. I'll give him a hand gesture. And I'll give it to him for free.'

> *John Prescott, on Iain Duncan Smith*

'The leader of the international criminal gang of bastards.'

> *Mohammed Saeed al-Sahaf, former Iraqi Information Minister, about George W. Bush*

'Those only deserve to be hit with shoes.'

> *Mohammed Saeed al-Sahaf, on George W. Bush and Donald Rumsfeld. He refers to the Iraqi insult of hitting enemies with footwear.*

'When we were making the law, when we were writing the literature and the mathematics, the grandfathers of Blair and little Bush were scratching around in caves.'

> *Mohammed Saeed al-Sahaf*

—— INSULTS AND PUTDOWNS ——

'Robin Cook's misfortune is to sound as if his voice never broke – but his behaviour encourages this view.'

> *Jacob Rees-Mogg, former Conservative MP, son of Lord Rees-Mogg*

'He can't help it. He was born with a silver foot in his mouth.'

> *Ann Richards, former Governor of Texas, on misstatements made by George Bush, Sr*

'I wouldn't vote for Ken Livingstone if he were running for Mayor of Toytown.'

> *Arthur Scargill, former President of the National Union of Mineworkers*

'I only play the Terminator; Tom Arnold married one.'

> *Arnold Schwarzenegger, actor and Governor of California, referring to Roseanne Barr*

—— INSULTS AND PUTDOWNS ——

'I just realised that I have a perfect part for you in Terminator 4.'

Arnold Schwarzenegger, during a televised debate with opponent Arianna Huffington, who called him a chauvinist

'Clearly, Bush lied. Now if he is an unconscious liar, and doesn't realise when he's lying, then we're really in trouble. Because, absolutely, it was a lie. They said they knew the weapons were there. He had members of the administration say they knew where the weapons were. So we're not just talking about something passing here. We're talking about 500 lives. We're talking about billions of dollars. So I hope he knew he was lying, because if he didn't, and just went in some kind of crazy, psychological breakdown, then we are really in trouble ... I'm a minister. Why do people lie? Because they're liars. He lied in Florida; he's lied several times. I believe he lied in Iraq ... Why he lied? I think we should give him the rest of his retirement to figure that out and explain to us.'

Al Sharpton, Reverend and US Presidential candidate, during a Democratic presidential debate

—— INSULTS AND PUTDOWNS ——

'He uses his charm to get what he wants. He is a media star. He thinks in soundbites.'

> *Clare Short, Labour MP and ex-Cabinet Minister, writing in the New Statesman about Tony Blair*

'You think you are big enough to make me, you little wimp? Come on, come over here and make me, I dare you ... You little fruitcake. You little fruitcake. I said you are a fruitcake.'

> *Peter Stark, US Democratic Representative for California, to Representative Scott McInnis, after McInnis told him to 'shut up' during a legislative dispute*

'I've met Boy Scouts with more military bearing.'

> *Norman Tebbit, former Conservative MP, on then Defence Secretary, Geoff Hoon*

'The Tory party will last. I don't know about Iain Duncan Smith, because we all die, but the party doesn't.'

> *Margaret Thatcher, former British Conservative Prime Minister*

—— INSULTS AND PUTDOWNS ——

'I never called Richard Nixon a son of a bitch;
after all, he claims to be a self-made man.'
Harry S. Truman, 33rd US President

'Richard Nixon is a no good, lying bastard.
He can lie out of both sides of his mouth at the
same time, and, if he ever caught himself telling
the truth, he'd lie just to keep his hand in.'
Harry S. Truman

'Harold Wilson is going around the country
stirring up apathy.'
*William Whitelaw, former Conservative MP and
Secretary of State for Northern Ireland*

5

PURE NONSENSE

PURE NONSENSE

'It contains a misleading impression, not a lie. It was being economical with the truth.'
Sir Robert Armstrong, Cabinet Secretary under Chamberlain and Heath

'I don't – sorry – I do not … the moment you ask me that question you immediately have the right to ask anyone that question and I do not accept the validity of the question.'
Paddy Ashdown, former Liberal Democrats leader

'There are two kinds of truth. There are real truths, and there are made-up truths.'
Marion Barry, former Mayor of Washington, D.C. on his arrest for drug use

'If I, taking care of everyone's interests, also take care of my own, you can't talk about a conflict of interest.'
Silvio Berlusconi, former Italian Prime Minister and simultaneously one of Italy's biggest tycoons, with major media holdings

———— PURE NONSENSE ————

'I find that whenever I am in power, or my father was in power, somehow good things happen. The economy picks up, we have good rains, water comes, people have crops. I think the reason this happens is that we want to give love and we receive love.'
Benazir Bhutto, former Prime Minister of Pakistan

'I didn't come into politics to change the Labour Party. I came into politics to change the country.'
Tony Blair, British Prime Minister

'One reason I changed the Labour Party is so that we can remain true to our principles.'
Tony Blair

"I have never told a lie,"
Tony Blair, on the truth

'We must watch our backs from those whose column inches, like maggots, rot the fruit of our endeavours from the inside out.'
David Blunkett, former Home Secretary, on the media

PURE NONSENSE

'George Bush was not elected by a majority of the voters in the United States. He was appointed by God.'

Lt. Gen. William Boykin, US Defence Undersecretary in charge of hunting down top terrorists in Iraq and Afghanistan

'We're going to move left and right at the same time.'

Jerry Brown, former Governor of California

'I'm sick of answering questions about the fucking peace process.'

John Bruton, former Irish Prime Minister

'The ambassador and the general were briefing me on the – the vast majority of Iraqis want to live in a peaceful, free world. And we will find these people and we will bring them to justice.'

George W. Bush, US President

─────── PURE NONSENSE ───────

'See, one of the interesting things in the Oval
Office – I love to bring people into the Oval
Office – right around the corner from here – and
say, this is where I office, but I want you to know
the office is always bigger than the person.'

George W. Bush

'I know what I believe. I will continue to
articulate what I believe and what I believe –
I believe what I believe is right.'

George W. Bush

'The true strength of America happens when a
neighbour loves a neighbour just like they'd
like to be loved themselves.'

George W. Bush

'Whether they be Christian, Jew, or Muslim, or
Hindu, people have heard the universal call to
love a neighbour just like they'd like to be
called themselves.'

George W. Bush

———————— PURE NONSENSE ————————

'The great thing about America is everybody should vote.'

George W. Bush

'We are fully committed to working with both sides to bring the level of terror down to an acceptable level for both.'

George W. Bush

'After all, a week ago, there were … Yasser Arafat was boarded up in his building in Ramallah, a building full of, evidently, German peace protestors and all kinds of people. They're now out. He's now free to show leadership, to lead the world.'

George W. Bush

—————— PURE NONSENSE ——————

'I'm a patient man. And when I say I'm a patient man, I mean I'm a patient man. Nothing he [Saddam Hussein] has done has convinced me – I'm confident the Secretary of Defence – that he is the kind of fellow that is willing to forgo weapons of mass destruction, is willing to be a peaceful neighbour, that is – will honour the people – the Iraqi people of all stripes, will – values human life. He hasn't convinced me, nor has he convinced my administration.'

George W. Bush

'I think we're making progress. We understand where the power of this country lay. It lays in the hearts and souls of Americans. It must lay in our pocketbooks. It lays in the willingness for people to work hard. But as importantly, it lays in the fact that we've got citizens from all walks of life, all political parties, that are willing to say, I want to love my neighbour. I want to make somebody's life just a little bit better.'

George W. Bush

—————— PURE NONSENSE ——————

'I have opinions of my own, strong opinions, but I don't always agree with them.'

George W. Bush

'There's a lot of people in the Middle East who are desirous to get into the Mitchell process. And – but first things first. The – these terrorist acts and, you know, the responses have got to end in order for us to get the framework – the groundwork, not framework – the groundwork to discuss a framework for peace, to lay the – all right.'

George W. Bush

'Actually, I – this may sound a little West Texas to you, but I like it. When I'm talking about – when I'm talking about myself, and when he's talking about myself, all of us are talking about me.'

George W. Bush

'The fact that he relies on facts – says things that are not factual – are going to undermine his campaign.'

George W. Bush

———————— PURE NONSENSE ————————

'I mean, these good folks are revolutionising how businesses conduct their business. And, like them, I am very optimistic about our position in the world and about its influence on the United States. We're concerned about the short-term economic news, but long-term I'm optimistic. And so, I hope investors, you know – secondly, I hope investors hold investments for periods of time – that I've always found the best investments are those that you salt away based on economics.'

George W. Bush

'What I am against is quotas. I am against hard quotas, quotas they basically delineate based upon whatever. However they delineate, quotas, I think, vulcanise society. So I don't know how that fits into what everybody else is saying, their relative positions, but that's my position.'

George W. Bush

——————— PURE NONSENSE ———————

'When I was coming up, it was a dangerous world, and you knew exactly who they were. It was us versus them, and it was clear who them was. Today we are not so sure who the they are, but we know they're there.'

George W. Bush

'Washington is a town where there's all kinds of allegations. You've heard much of the allegations. And if people have got solid information, please come forward with it. And that would be people inside the information who are the so-called anonymous sources, or people outside the information – outside the administration.'

George W. Bush

'There's only one person who hugs the mothers and the widows, the wives and the kids upon the death of their loved one. Others hug, but having committed the troops, I've got an additional responsibility to hug and that's me and I know what it's like.'

George W. Bush

———— PURE NONSENSE ————

'I will have a foreign-handed foreign policy.'
George W. Bush

'As you know, these are open forums, you're
able to come and listen to what I have to say.'
George W. Bush

'One of the common denominators I have
found is that expectations rise above that which
is expected.'
George W. Bush

'Well, it's an unimaginable honour to be the
president during the Fourth of July of this
country. It means what these words say, for
starters. The great inalienable rights of our
country. We're blessed with such values in
America. And I – it's – I'm a proud man
to be the nation based upon such wonderful
values.'
George W. Bush

—————— PURE NONSENSE ——————

'I think, if you know what you believe, it makes it a lot easier to answer questions. I can't answer your question.'

George W. Bush, in response to a question about whether he wished he could take back any of his answers in the first debate

'First, we would not accept a treaty that would not have been ratified, nor a treaty that I thought made sense for the country.'

George W. Bush

'Now, we talked to Joan Hanover. She and her husband, George, were visiting with us. They are near retirement – retiring – in the process of retiring, meaning they're very smart, active, capable people who are retirement age and are retiring.'

George W. Bush

'I think we need not only to eliminate the tollbooth to the middle class, I think we should knock down the tollbooth.'

George W. Bush

PURE NONSENSE

'For every fatal shooting, there were roughly three non-fatal shootings. And, folks, this is unacceptable in America. It's just unacceptable. And we're going to do something about it.'
George W. Bush.

'If a person doesn't have the capacity that we all want that person to have, I suspect hope is in the far distant future, if at all.'
George W. Bush

'I don't bring God into my life to – to, you know, kind of be a political person.'
George W. Bush

'In other words, I don't think people ought to be compelled to make the decision which they think is best for their family.'
George W. Bush

——— PURE NONSENSE ———

'I knew it might put him in an awkward position that we had a discussion before finality has finally happened in this presidential race.'
George W. Bush, describing a phonecall
to Senator John Breaux

'It's important for us to explain to our nation that life is important. It's not only life of babies, but it's life of children living in, you know, the dark dungeons of the Internet.'
George W. Bush

'Sometimes, Washington is one of these towns where the person – people who think they've got the sharp elbow is the most effective person.'
George W. Bush

'We've had leaks out of the administrative branch, had leaks out of the legislative branch, and out of the executive branch and the legislative branch, and I've spoken out consistently against them, and I want to know who the leakers are.'
George W. Bush

—————— PURE NONSENSE ——————

'But the true threats to stability and peace are these nations that are not very transparent, that hide behind the – that don't let people in to take a look and see what they're up to. They're very kind of authoritarian regimes. The true threat is whether or not one of these people decide, peak of anger, try to hold us hostage, ourselves; the Israelis, for example, to whom we'll defend, offer our defences; the South Koreans.'

George W. Bush

'If affirmative action means what I just described, what I'm for, then I'm for it.'

George W. Bush

'See, we love – we love freedom. That's what they didn't understand. They hate things; we love things. They act out of hatred; we don't seek revenge, we seek justice out of love.'

George W. Bush

—————— PURE NONSENSE ——————

'Our country puts $1 billion a year up to help feed the hungry. And we're by far the most generous nation in the world when it comes to that, and I'm proud to report that. This isn't a contest of who's the most generous. I'm just telling you as an aside. We're generous. We shouldn't be bragging about it. But we are. We're very generous.'

George W. Bush

'That's a chapter, the last chapter of the 20th, 20th, the 21st century that most of us would rather forget. The last chapter of the 20th century. This is the first chapter of the 21st century.'

George W. Bush, on the Monica Lewinsky scandal

'Listen, Al Gore is a very tough opponent. He is the incumbent. He represents the incumbency. And a challenger is somebody who generally comes from the pack and wins, if you're going to win. And that's where I'm coming from.'

George W. Bush

———————— PURE NONSENSE ————————

'You've also got to measure in order to begin to effect change that's just more – when there's more than talk, there's just actual – a paradigm shift.'

George W. Bush

'Oftentimes, we live in a processed world – you know, people focus on the process and not results.'

George W. Bush

'Then I went for a run with the other dog and just walked. And I started thinking about a lot of things. I was able to – I can't remember what it was. Oh, the inaugural speech, started thinking through that.'

George W. Bush

———— PURE NONSENSE ————

'We've got pockets of persistent poverty in our society, which I refuse to declare defeat – I mean, I refuse to allow them to continue on. And so one of the things that we're trying to do is to encourage a faith-based initiative to spread its wings all across America, to be able to capture this great compassionate spirit.'

George W. Bush

'All up and down the different aspects of our society, we had meaningful discussions. Not only in the Cabinet Room, but prior to this and after this day, our secretaries, respective secretaries, will continue to interact to create the conditions necessary for prosperity to reign.'

George W. Bush

'There's no cave deep enough for America, or dark enough to hide.'

George W. Bush

—————— PURE NONSENSE ——————

'Now, like, I'm President. It would be pretty hard for some drug guy to come into the White House and start offering it up, you know? ... I bet if they did, I hope I would say, "Hey, get lost. We don't want any of that."'

George Bush, Sr, 41st US President, speaking to a group of students about drug abuse

'You cannot be president of the United States if you don't have faith. Remember Lincoln, going to his knees in times of trial and the Civil War and all that stuff. You can't be. And we are blessed. So don't feel sorry for – don't cry for me, Argentina. Message: I care.'

George Bush, Sr

'Please don't ask me to do that which I've just said I'm not going to do, because you're burning up time. The meter is running through the sand on you, and I am now filibustering.'

George Bush, Sr

'I'm for a stronger death penalty.'

George Bush, Sr

—————— PURE NONSENSE ——————

A proof is a proof. What kind of a proof? It's a proof. A proof is a proof. And when you have a good proof, it's because it's proven.
  Jean Chretien, former Canadian Prime Minister

'We have no political prisoners, only communists and others involved in conspiracies against the country.'
  Park Chung-Lee, former South Korean President

'The more killings and homicides you have, the more havoc it prevents.'
  Richard M Daley, Mayor of Chicago

'We know smoking tobacco is not good for kids, but a lot of other things aren't good. Drinking's not good. Some would say milk's not good.'
  Bob Dole, former US Senator and Presidential Candidate

'The Government will never accept an acceptable level of violence.'
  Patrick Donegan, Irish politician

—————— PURE NONSENSE ——————

'Heterosexual intercourse is the pure, formalised expression of contempt for women's bodies.'
Andrea Dworkin, feminist writer

'We are not at war with Egypt. We are in an armed conflict.'
Anthony Eden, former British Conservative Prime Minister

'The world is more like it is now than it ever was before.'
Dwight D. Eisenhower, 34th US President

'Things happen more frequently in the future than they do in the past.'
Booth Gardner, former Governor of Washington

—————— PURE NONSENSE ——————

'The theories – the ideas she expressed about equality of results within legislative bodies and with – by outcome, by decisions made by legislative bodies, ideas related to proportional voting as a general remedy, not in particular cases where the circumstances make that a feasible idea ...'

Al Gore, former US Vice-President

'What a waste it is to lose one's mind. Or not to have a mind is being very wasteful. How true that is.'

Al Gore

'The American people would not want to know of any misquotes that Al Gore may or may not make.'

Al Gore

'Two things are absolutely clear and I want to make them absolutely clear.'

Harriet Harman, Labour MP

———————— PURE NONSENSE ————————

'My general approach is that you mustn't
generalise.'

Harriet Harman

'I think if we didn't know about it, we wouldn't
know whether we didn't know about it.'
*Harriet Harman, talking about US-led rendition
flights, which allegedly move terrorist suspects
from domestic or ally soil to countries where
torture is legally practiced to acquire
information from them*

'Capital punishment is our society's recognition
of the sanctity of human life.'

Orrin Hatch, US Senator for Utah

'No bystanders, no snipers from the sidelines.
Every one of us a fully engaged participant in
the great battle of hearts and minds and ideas.'
*Michael Howard, former Conservative leader,
outlining his vision for the Conservative Party*

——————— PURE NONSENSE ———————

'As I've said before and I said yesterday, this is one of the key questions that will be decided or not decided at Edinburgh.'

Lord Douglas Hurd, former Conservative MP and Home Secretary

'It is enough to have grenades, launchers, a loaf of bread, a drink of water and a rifle. Then, counting on God, Iraq will be safe.'

Saddam Hussein, former President of Iraq

'I am proud to have been born fearing God and I have taught my children the value of history and the value of human stands.'

Saddam Hussein, speaking on CBS television

'Working mothers are the backbone of the third half of the economy.'

Glenda Jackson, Labour MP

'What we go into the next general election with may not obviously make sense in terms of what we were saying at a previous general election.'

Charles Kennedy, former Liberal Democrat leader

—————— PURE NONSENSE ——————

'Life is indeed precious, and I think the death penalty helps to affirm this fact.'
Ed Koch, former Mayor of New York City

'I do not like the word bomb. It is not a bomb. It is a device which is exploding.'
Jacques Le Blanc, former French Ambassador to New Zealand, on nuclear testing in France

'If I invade Mars, the Labour Party will invade Mars. From their point of view, Mars today, Cadbury tomorrow and Bourneville the day after. Heaven knows where they will go next.'
John Major, former British Conservative Prime Minister

'I am not denying anything I did not say.'
Brian Mulroney, former Canadian Prime Minister

'I was not lying. I said things that later on seemed to be untrue.'
Richard Nixon, 37th US President

———— PURE NONSENSE ————

'I was provided with additional input that was radically different from the truth. I assisted in furthering that version.'

Colonel Oliver North, former US Counter-Terrorism Coordinator, from his Iran-Contra testimony

'The United States, which has a similar type of voting system as ourselves, but very different ...'

David Owen, MP

'All have a contributory contribution to congestion.'

John Prescott, Deputy Prime Minister

'My position is that I want to make our position clear ... the example in Germany is just one example, for example.'

John Prescott

'The global alliance I'm calling for is as much for peace as well as war, and these two things need to be done if we're to sort out this problem.'

John Prescott

—————— PURE NONSENSE ——————

"The objectives remain the same and indeed that has been made clear by the Prime Minister in a speech yesterday that the objectives are clear and the one about the removal of the Taliban is not something we have as a clear objective to implement but it is possible a consequence that will flow from the Taliban clearly giving protection to Bin Laden and the UN resolution made it absolutely clear that anyone that finds them in that position declares themselves an enemy and that clearly is a matter for these objectives."

John Prescott

'I'm asking you, if I gave you these facts, you're supposed to give some factual analysis to it – I mean, you're not denying that these facts are wrong, are you?'

John Prescott

'That's precisely try now and more so this four more years on.'

John Prescott

————— PURE NONSENSE —————

'We shall make a decisive decision.'

John Prescott

'We'll let the sunshine in and shine on us,
because today we're happy and tomorrow we'll
be even happier.'

Dan Quayle, former US Vice-President

'It isn't pollution that's harming the
environment. It's the impurities in our air and
water that are doing it.'

Dan Quayle

'... getting [cruise missiles] more accurate so
that we can have precise precision.'

Dan Quayle

'I deserve respect for the things I did not do.'

Dan Quayle

'I stand by all the misstatements that I've made.'

Dan Quayle

—————— PURE NONSENSE ——————

'I feel that this [1981] is my first year, that next year is an election year, that the third year is the midpoint and that the fourth year is the last chance I'll have to make a record since the last two years, I'll be a candidate again. Everything I do in those last two years will be posturing for the election. But right now I don't have to do that.'

Dan Quayle

'El Salvador is a democracy so it's not surprising that there are many voices to be heard here. Yet in my conversations with Salvadorans ... I have heard a single voice.'

Dan Quayle

'James Bond is a man of honour, a symbol of real value to the free world.'

Ronald Reagan, 40th US President

'I with myself saw what the soldiers in Bosnia were doing.'

Malcolm Rifkind, former Conservative MP

—————— PURE NONSENSE ——————

'I concluded from the beginning that this would be the end, and I am right, for it is not half over yet.'

Boyle Roche, 18th- century Member of Parliament from Tralee

'Their military uniforms were all different – chiefly green.'

Boyle Roche

'I should have answered your letter a fortnight ago, but I only received it this morning.'

Boyle Roche

'Immediately every man in the place, including women and children, ran out to meet them.'

Boyle Roche

'At present, there are such goings on in Ireland that everything is at a standstill.'

Boyle Roche

PURE NONSENSE

'An alarm was given that a gang of rebels in full retreat were advancing under the French standard. They had no colours nor any drums except bagpipes.'

Boyle Roche

'The only way to prevent what's past is to put a stop to it before it happens.'

Boyle Roche

'I can smell a rat. I can see him floating in the air, but mark me – I shall nip him in the bud.'

Boyle Roche

'I believe in preventing unnecessary crime.'
Angela Rumbold, 1997 Conservative candidate

'Freedom is untidy.'
Donald Rumsfeld, US Defence Secretary commenting on the looting that went on in Baghdad after the invasion of Iraq in 2003

—————— PURE NONSENSE ——————

'Reports that say that something hasn't happened are always interesting to me, because, as we know, there are known knowns; there are things we know we know. We also know there are known unknowns; that is to say we know there are some things we do not know. But there are also unknown unknowns – the ones we don't know we don't know.'

Donald Rumsfeld

'I would not say that the future is necessarily less predictable than the past. I think the past was not predictable when it started.'

Donald Rumsfeld

'I believe what I said yesterday. I don't know what I said, but I know what I think, and, well, I assume it's what I said.'

Donald Rumsfeld

'Well, um, you know, something's neither good nor bad but thinking makes it so, I suppose, as Shakespeare said.'

Donald Rumsfeld

──────── PURE NONSENSE ────────

'If I said yes, that would then suggest that that might be the only place where it might be done which would not be accurate, necessarily accurate. It might also not be inaccurate, but I'm disinclined to mislead anyone.'

Donald Rumsfeld, when he was questioned about training and equipping Iraqi opposition

'There's another way to phrase that and that is that the absence of evidence is not the evidence of absence. It is basically saying the same thing in a different way. Simply because you do not have evidence that something does exist does not mean that you have evidence that it doesn't exist.'

Donald Rumsfeld

'All of a sudden, we see riots, we see protests, we see people clashing. The next thing we know, there is injured or there is dead people. We don't want to get to that extent.'

Arnold Schwarzenegger, actor and Governor of California, on the dangers posed by gay marriage

PURE NONSENSE

'Gaiety is the most outstanding feature of the Soviet Union'

Joseph Stalin, leader of the Soviet Union

'I can't speak for Arab journalists, but British journalists are perfect.'

Jack Straw, Labour MP and Leader of the Commons, when told by his Libyan counterpart that his country's actions had been distorted in the Arab press

"Because it was quite dark in that corner I was being pushed towards shaking hands with somebody just as a matter of courtesy and then it transpired it was President Mugabe."

Jack Straw

'In the case of my own case, this has not been the case.'

Peter Tatchell, gay rights activist

———— PURE NONSENSE ————

'War is a biological necessity of the first importance.'

Friedrich von Bernhardt, Nazi General,
speaking in 1910

'Now the only thing that remains unresolved is the resolution of the problem.'
Tom Wells, former Ontario Education Minister

'Those who say that I am not in agreement with the policy are, rightly or wrongly, quite wrong.'
William Whitelaw, former Conservative MP and
Secretary of State for Northern Ireland

'I can assure you that I definitely might take action.'

William Whitelaw

'There are sometimes good reasons why young people need, and can benefit from, proper and controlled access to firearms – for example, if they are growing up on a farm.'

Ann Widdecombe, Conservative MP

6

BLUNDERS AND GAFFES

——— BLUNDERS AND GAFFES ———

'Its nice to be in Devon again.'
*Paddy Ashdown, former Liberal Democrats
leader in Cornwall*

'I tried to tell the French Prime Minister in
French that I admired the various positions he
had taken on so many matters. What I actually
said was that I desired the French Prime
Minister in many positions.'
Tony Blair, British Prime Minister

'The single most important two things we can do.'
Tony Blair

'I was very confident we would find them. I
have to accept we have not found them. I have
to accept we may not find them.'
Tony Blair on weapons of mass destruction

'It is important for Britain and France to work
closer together and, of course, our relationship
with Germany is immensely important.'
*Tony Blair, welcoming German Chancellor
Angela Merkel*

—— BLUNDERS AND GAFFES ——

'I haven't got a clue.'

> *David Blunkett, former Home Secretary,*
> *when questioned about the number of*
> *unregistered migrants in Britain*

'This is Preservation Month. I appreciate preservation. It's what you do when you run for president. You gotta preserve.'

> *George W. Bush, US President, speaking at*
> *Fairgrounds Elementary School in Nashua, New*
> *Hampshire, during 'Perseverance Month'*

'There's Adam Clymer, major league asshole from the New York Times.'

> *George W. Bush, to his running mate Dick*
> *Cheney, just before a campaign speech in Illinois*

'I regret that a private comment I made to the Vice Presidential candidate made it through the public airways.'

> *George W. Bush, on his*
> *'major league asshole' remark*

—————— BLUNDERS AND GAFFES ——————

'We've had a great weekend here in the Land of the Enchanted.'

George W. Bush, during a visit to New Mexico – the state's nickname is 'Land of Enchantment'

'The war on terror involves Saddam Hussein because of the nature of Saddam Hussein, the history of Saddam Hussein, and his willingness to terrorise himself.'

George W. Bush

'The trial lawyers are very politically powerful ... But here in Texas we took them on and got some good medical – medical malpractice.'

George W. Bush

'Over 75 per cent of white Americans own their home, and less than 50 per cent of Hispanos and African Americans don't own their home. And that's a gap, that's a homeownership gap. And we've got to do something about it.'

George W. Bush

—— BLUNDERS AND GAFFES ——

'When Iraq is liberated, you will be treated, tried and persecuted as a war criminal.'

> *George W. Bush, to Saddam Hussein.*
> *Mr Bush probably intended to say*
> *'prosecuted' instead of 'persecuted'*

'We'll let our friends be the peacekeepers and the great country called America will be the pacemakers.'

> *George W. Bush*

'Earlier today, the Libyan Government released Fathi Jahmi. She's a local government official who was imprisoned in 2002 for advocating free speech and democracy.'

> *George W. Bush, referring to Jahmi, a man, in a*
> *speech paying tribute to women reformers*
> *during International Women's Week*

'There's an old saying in Tennessee – I know it's in Texas, probably in Tennessee –that says, fool me once, shame on – shame on you. Fool me – you can't get fooled again.'

> *George W. Bush*

—— BLUNDERS AND GAFFES ——

'I am pleased to have the responsibility of being President of the United States. As young Americans you also have an important responsibility, which is to become good citizens.'

George W. Bush, in a letter to a group of schoolchildren in Lancashire, in the UK

'We're concerned about AIDS inside our White House – make no mistake about it.'

George W. Bush

'You're free. And freedom is beautiful. And, you know, it'll take time to restore chaos and order – order out of chaos. But we will.'

George W. Bush

'One year ago today, the time for excuse-making has come to an end.'

George W. Bush

——— BLUNDERS AND GAFFES ———

'The goals for this country are peace in the world. And the goals for this country are a compassionate American for every single citizen. That compassion is found in the hearts and souls of the American citizens.'

George W. Bush

'I am here to make an announcement that this Thursday, ticket counters and airplanes will fly out of Ronald Reagan Airport.'

George W. Bush

'My administration has been calling upon all the leaders in the – in the Middle East to do everything they can to stop the violence, to tell the different parties involved that peace will never happen.'

George W. Bush

'John Thune has got a common-sense vision for good forest policy. I look forward to working with him in the United Nations Senate to preserve these national heritages.'

George W. Bush

─── BLUNDERS AND GAFFES ───

'Any time we've got any kind of inkling that somebody is thinking about doing something to an American and something to our homeland, you've just got to know we're moving on it, to protect the United Nations Constitution, and at the same time, we're protecting you.'

George W. Bush

'I need to be able to move the right people to the right place at the right time to protect you, and I'm not going to accept a lousy bill out of the United Nations Senate.'

George W. Bush

'I think the American people – I hope the American – I don't think, let me – I hope the American people trust me.'

George W. Bush

'There's no such thing as legacies. At least, there is a legacy, but I'll never see it.'

George W. Bush

——— BLUNDERS AND GAFFES ———

'I suspect that had my dad not been President, he'd be asking the same questions: How'd your meeting go with so-and-so? ... How did you feel when you stood up in front of the people for the State of the Union Address – state of the budget address, whatever you call it.'

George W. Bush

'I was proud the other day when both Republicans and Democrats stood with me in the Rose Garden to announce their support for a clear statement of purpose: you disarm, or we will.'

George W. Bush, on Iraq

'It's amazing I won. I was running against peace, prosperity and incumbency.'

George W. Bush, speaking to Swedish Prime Minister Goran Perrson, unaware that a live television camera was still rolling

'It would be a mistake for the United States Senate to allow any kind of human cloning to come out of that chamber.'

George W. Bush

BLUNDERS AND GAFFES

'I urge the leaders in Europe and around the world to take swift, decisive action against terror groups such as Hamas, to cut off their funding, and to support – cut funding and support, as the United States has done.'

George W. Bush

'We had a chance to visit with Teresa Nelson who's a parent, and a mom or a dad.'

George W. Bush

'Neither in French nor in English nor in Mexican.'

George W. Bush, refusing to take reporters' questions during a photo call with then Canadian Prime Minister Jean Chretien

'Then you wake up at the high school level and find out that the illiteracy level of our children are appalling.'

George W. Bush

——— BLUNDERS AND GAFFES ———

'One of the most meaningful things that's happened to me since I've been the Governor – the President – Governor – President. Oops. Ex-Governor. I went to Bethesda Naval Hospital to give a fellow a Purple Heart, and at the same moment I watched him – get a Purple Heart for action in Iraq – and at that same – right after I gave him the Purple Heart, he was sworn in as a citizen of the United States – a Mexican citizen, now a United States citizen.'

George W. Bush

'And so, in my State of the – my State of the Union – or state – my speech to the nation, whatever you want to call it, speech to the nation – I asked Americans to give 4,000 years – 4,000 hours over the next – the rest of your life – of service to America. That's what I asked – 4,000 hours.'

George W. Bush

'And, most importantly, Alma Powell, secretary of Colin Powell, is with us.'

George W. Bush

——— BLUNDERS AND GAFFES ———

'For seven and a half years I've worked alongside President Reagan. We've had triumphs, made some mistakes. We've had some sex – uh, setbacks.'

George Bush, Sr, 41st US President

'You are a worthy representative of the new democracy in Brazil.'

James Callaghan, former British Labour Prime Minister, to the President of Portugal

"To his majesty the King of Sweden!'

James Callaghan, toasting the King of Norway

'I have said that I am not running and I'm having a great time being Pres– being a first-term senator.'

Hillary Clinton, on her lack of ambition to become President

'I will never forget the '81 – or was it '82? – honours list.'

Julian Critchley, former Conservative MP

——— BLUNDERS AND GAFFES ———

'You read what Disraeli had to say. I don't remember what he said. He said something. He's no longer with us.'

>*Bob Dole, former US Senator and*
>*Presidential candidate*

'Our intent will not be to create gridlock. Oh, except maybe from time to time.'

>*Bob Dole*

'I intend to open the country up to democracy, and anyone who is against that I will jail, I will crush.'

>*Joao Figueiredo, former Brazilian President*

'When my sister and I were growing up, there was never any doubt in our minds that men and women were equal, if not more so.'

>*Al Gore, former US Vice President,*
>*to a group of women*

'There's a lot of overcrowded prisons in the south, and we're planning a new one.'

>*Douglas Hurd, former Conservative MP and*
>*Home Secretary*

—— BLUNDERS AND GAFFES ——

'Homelessness is homelessness no matter where you live.'

Glenda Jackson, Labour MP

'She's a wonderful, wonderful person, and we're looking to a happy and wonderful night – ah, life.'

Ted Kennedy, US Senator, speaking about his then fiancée, Victoria Reggie

'This is a great day for France!'

Richard Nixon, 37th US President, while attending Charles De Gaulle's funeral

'The green belt is a Labour policy, and we intend to build on it.'

John Prescott, Deputy Prime Minister

'It is wonderful to be here in the great state of Chicago.'

Dan Quayle, former US Vice-President

'I'm Dan Quayle. Who are you?'

Dan Quayle, to his Secret Service agent

—— BLUNDERS AND GAFFES ——

'Certainly, I know what to do, and when I am
Vice-President – and I will be – there will be
contingency plans under different sets of
situations and I tell you what, I'm not going to
go out and hold a news conference about it. I'm
going to put it in a safe and keep it there! Does
that answer your question?'

*Dan Quayle, when asked what he would do if he
assumed the Presidency*

'We expect them [Salvadoran officials] to work
toward the elimination of human rights.'

Dan Quayle

'The real question for 1988 is whether we're
going to go forward to tomorrow or past to
the – to the back!'

Dan Quayle

'I happen to be a Republican President, ah, the
Vice-President.'

Dan Quayle

—— BLUNDERS AND GAFFES ——

'The President is going to lead us out of this recovery. It will happen.'

> *Dan Quayle, on the campaign trail.*

'Republicans understand the importance of bondage between a mother and child.'

> *Dan Quayle*

'Gerald Ford was a Communist.'

> *Ronald Reagan, 40th US President, in a speech.*
> *He meant to say 'Congressman'*

'My fellow Americans, I've signed legislation that will outlaw Russia forever. We begin bombing in five minutes.'

> *Ronald Reagan, before a scheduled*
> *radio broadcast, unaware that the*
> *microphone was already on*

'This is really embarrassing. I just forgot our state governor's name, but I know that you will help me recall him.'

> *Ronald Reagan, speaking to a*
> *taxpayer advocacy group*

—— BLUNDERS AND GAFFES ——

'Now we are trying to get unemployment to go up, and I think we are going to succeed.'
Ronald Reagan, in 1982

'The United States has much to offer the third world war.'
Ronald Reagan. He meant to say 'the Third World'.

'You too have difficulties with unemployment in the United States.'
Ronald Reagan, speaking in Canada

'The Jews and Arabs should sit down and settle their differences like good Christians.'
Warren Robinson Austin, former US politician, on problems in the Middle East

7

WITTY AND WISE
POLITICIANS

—WITTY AND WISE POLITICIANS—

'I do go to church regularly. And of course I confess my sins, but that's between Him and me.'

> Gerry Adams, President of Sinn Fein,
> when asked if he goes to church

'It is hard to argue with the government. Remember, they run the Bureau of Alcohol, Tobacco, and Firearms, so they must know a thing or two about satisfying women.'

> Scott Adams, humourist

'I realise I am as welcome in the Tory party as Banquo's ghost.'

> Jonathan Aitken, disgraced former
> Conservative MP, jailed for perjury, who wants
> to run for election again

'Of all the nine Parliaments I have been in, it is the most boring, bland, uncontroversial, sycophantic, tedious, yawn-making assembly ever housed under the roof at Westminster.'

> Joe Ashton, Labour MP, on the
> current Parliament

—WITTY AND WISE POLITICIANS—

'Greg Pope, the current Labour MP for
Hyndburn, Lancashire, swears that his name
printed on the ballot paper as "Pope Gregory"
is worth a thousand votes from Catholic old
dears all over the constituency.'

Joe Ashton

'Television is an idiot's lantern.'

*Clement Attlee, former British
Labour Prime Minister*

'Lloyd George spent his whole life plastering
together the true and false and therefrom
manufacturing the plausible.'

*Stanley Baldwin, former British
Conservative Prime Minister*

'I didn't actually find many facts, but I had a
good time'

*Tony Banks, MP, former Sports Minister, on a
recent fact-finding mission to Japan*

—WITTY AND WISE POLITICIANS—

"In over 50 years of political life, I have learned at least one valuable lesson: 'If anyone offers to resign in a huff, accept!' It saves time,"
Lord Beaumont of Whitley, Green Party peer

'It's a product whose benefits you are not quite sure of, a bit old fashioned, and not popular enough for you to want to tell your friends that you use it.'
Lord Bell, Conservative peer,
regarding the question of how to
make the Tory party electable

'You'll have to ask God when I'm going.'
Lord Bell, Chairman of Chime Communications,
on when he will retire

'I am the party as well as its leader, which can save a fortune. I hold my party conferences three times a year, they last two hours and I buy all the drinks.'
Martin Bell, former Independent MP

—WITTY AND WISE POLITICIANS—

'If capitalism depended on the intellectual quality of the Conservative Party, it would end about lunchtime tomorrow.'
Tony Benn, former Labour MP

"The invitation could be: come and die in Italy.'
Silvio Berlusconi, former Italian Prime Minister,
on Rome scrapping inheritance tax

'I sometimes think modern politics is a conspiracy against understanding.'
Tony Blair, British Prime Minister

'If I could get even a tenth as much publicity for the primary results in our schools as I did for my shirt, I'd be a lucky man.'
Tony Blair, on his sweaty shirt
at the Labour conference

'It is about the only thing I have done that any of my kids have considered worthy of comment.'
Tony Blair, on his appearance on
The Simpsons

—WITTY AND WISE POLITICIANS—

"I almost lost your vote there by saying you sounded Australian"
> *Tony Blair speaking to a New Zealander*
> *during a walkabout*

'It is a masterstroke by the organisers to site the beach volleyball in Horse Guards Parade just outside the Prime Minister's window.'
> *Tony Blair, launching Britain's*
> *2012 Olympic bid*

'If this is New Labour, why do I feel so old?'
> *Tony Blair*

'You don't need a guide dog for hindsight.'
> *David Blunkett, former Home Secretary*

'Here I am, the so-called "hard man", the unbending Home Secretary, and a dog can bring tears to my eyes.'
> *David Blunkett, on his relationship*
> *with his guide dog*

—WITTY AND WISE POLITICIANS—

'When I see the checkout girls at Sainsbury's breastfeeding at the till, I might agree to give it some thought.'

> *Betty Boothroyd, former Speaker, on her ban on breastfeeding in the Commons*

'I can have objections to instruments that merely vibrate.'

> *Betty Boothroyd*

'With the early finishes in the evenings, it was either sex, drugs or rock and roll, and since we can't do the sex and drugs it had to be rock and roll'

> *Labour MP Kevin Brennan, on forming a pop group with other MPs*

'What do you call a Tory candidate whose name begins with "A"? The accused.'

> *Gordon Brown, Chancellor of the Exchequer*

—WITTY AND WISE POLITICIANS—

'I hope the Spice Girls will come back, although it may be beyond even Bob Geldof to get that to happen.'

Gordon Brown

'Nothing beats Reaganomics: though herpes runs it close.'

Art Buchwald, author, columnist, dramatist and journalist

'Oh yeah, the guy who came with the runner.'

George W. Bush, US President, on William Hague, who met him with Sebastian Coe, his chief of staff

'One of the great things about books is sometimes there are some fantastic pictures.'

George W. Bush

'This foreign policy stuff is a little frustrating.'

George W. Bush

—WITTY AND WISE POLITICIANS—

'A dictatorship would be a heck of a lot easier, there's no question about it.'

George W. Bush

'My answer is bring them on.'

George W. Bush, on Iraqi militants attacking US forces

'It was pointed out to me that the last noted American to visit London stayed in a glass box dangling over the Thames. A few might have been happy to provide similar arrangements for me. I thank Her Majesty the Queen for interceding. We are honoured to be staying at her house.'

George W. Bush, during his State visit to the United Kingdom. The glass box referred to is that of David Blaine, the magician

'We both use Colgate toothpaste.'

George W. Bush, in February 2001, in response to the question of what he and Tony Blair might have in common

—WITTY AND WISE POLITICIANS—

"There is an iconic figure from the 1970s and 1980s that should inspire the Conservative party this week. I am of course referring to the hairy godfather of punk rock who recently died of cancer, Joey Ramone."

> *David Cameron, then a Conservative potential leader making his debut speech in the House of Commons in 2001*

'I have the most corny CV possible. It goes: Eton, Oxford, Conservative Research Department, Treasury, Home Office, Carlton TV and then Conservative MP.'

> *David Cameron, Conservative leader*

'I don't miss the limos and the jets. I do miss … What do I miss? I do miss Tony.'

> *Alastair Campbell, former Labour spin doctor in the Prime Minister's office*

—WITTY AND WISE POLITICIANS—

'There are not many areas in politics where
sitting on the fence is the right approach. But a
US presidential election, for a British Prime
Minister, is one of them.'

Alastair Campbell, Tony Blair's
former press secretary

'We don't do God. I'm sorry. We don't do God.'
Alastair Campbell, when American reporter
David Margolick asked about Tony Blair's
religious views

"You can lose the vote if you fail to close
the gate,"
Sir Menzies Campbelll, leader of the Liberal
Democrats, on the distribution of leaflets

'I have often wanted to drown my troubles,
but I can't get my wife to go swimming.'
Jimmy Carter, 39th US President

—WITTY AND WISE POLITICIANS—

'Here's an unsigned question. "Mr Vice-
President, don't you think it's time to step down
and let someone else add new energy and
vitality to the ticket?" No ... I don't. And, Rudy
[Giuliani], you need to do a better job
disguising your handwriting.'

Dick Cheney, Vice-President,
at the Gridiron Dinner

'When I get to Heaven I mean to spend a
considerable portion of my first million years in
painting, and so get to the bottom of the
subject.'

Winston Churchill, former British Prime Minister

'I do not know the location of the Virgin Islands
but at least I know that they are on the other
side of the world from Maidenhead.'

Winston Churchill

'One of my ministers found half-naked with a
guardsman in Hyde Park? Last Wednesday?
The coldest night of the year? Makes you proud
to be British.'

Winston Churchill

—WITTY AND WISE POLITICIANS—

'Yes, Mrs Braddock, I am drunk. But you, Mrs Braddock, are ugly, and disgustingly fat. But, tomorrow morning, I, Winston Churchill, will be sober.'

Winston Churchill

'I wrote my name at the top of the page. I wrote down the number of the question, 1. After much reflection, I put a bracket round it thus: "(1)". But thereafter I could not think of anything connected with it that was either relevant or true. It was from these slender indications of scholarship that Mr Weldon drew the conclusion that I was worthy to pass into Harrow. It was very much to his credit.'

Winston Churchill

'Sir Redvers Buller plodded from blunder to blunder and from one disaster to another, without losing either the regard of his country or the trust of his troops, to whose feeding as well as his own he paid serious attention.'

Winston Churchill

—WITTY AND WISE POLITICIANS—

'At every crisis the Kaiser crumpled. In defeat he fled; in revolution he abdicated; in exile he remarried.'

Winston Churchill

'When Ministers of the Crown speak like this on behalf of HM Government, the Prime Minister and his friends have no need to wonder why they are getting increasingly into bad odour. I have even asked myself, when meditating upon these points, whether you, Mr Speaker, would admit the word "lousy" as a Parliamentary expression in referring to the Administration, provided, of course, it was not intended in a contemptuous sense but purely as one of factual narration.'

Winston Churchill, responding to Minister of Fuel and Power Hugh Gaitskell's statement advocating saving energy by taking fewer baths

"It is impossible to obtain a conviction for sodomy from an English jury. Half of them don't believe that it can physically be done, and the other half are doing it."

Winston Churchill

—WITTY AND WISE POLITICIANS—

'The trick is not to live off the interest on one's capital, but off the interest on the interest.'
Alan Clark, former Conservative MP

'There are three things in this world you can do nothing about. Getting AIDS, getting clamped, and running out of Chateau Lafite "45".'
Alan Clark

'Eton was an early introduction to human cruelty, treachery and extreme physical hardship.'
Alan Clark

'Everyone in public life should be arrested at least once. It's an education.'
Alan Clark

'I have so many skeletons in the cupboard I can hardly shut the door.'
Alan Clark

IS IT JUST ME OR ARE ALL POLITICIANS SHITE?

—WITTY AND WISE POLITICIANS—

'I believe John Gotti wears $2,000 suits. I didn't
know it was possible to buy one so cheaply.'
Alan Clark

'I do not under any circumstances discuss my
relations with the ladies. I am a gentleman, not
a hairdresser.'
Alan Clark

'America is the only nation in history which
miraculously has gone directly from barbarism
to degeneration without the usual interval of
civilisation.'
George Clemenceau, former French politician

'When the Republicans had the White House
for 12 years, from 1980 to 1992, they took credit
every time the sun came up in the morning.'
Bill Clinton, 42nd US President

'They remind me of teenagers who got their
inheritance too soon and couldn't wait to blow it.'
Bill Clinton, on the Bush administration

—WITTY AND WISE POLITICIANS—

'You know, if I were a single man, I might ask
that mummy out. That's a good-looking mummy!'
*Bill Clinton, on the recently discovered
Inca mummy 'Juanita'*

'You know what's wrong with this country?
Everyone gets a chance to have their fair say.'
Bill Clinton

'I think I would be well advised to avoid any
discussion of promiscuity and whipping.'
*Robin Cook, Former Foreign Secretary and
Leader of the House of Commons, after having
been told that many MPs had lost their 'political
virginity' during the Iraq vote*

'Everyone now knows that there is a far better
chance of us discovering Beagle 2 on Mars
than ever finding weapons of mass destruction.'
Robin Cook, on Iraq

'It may be Valentine's Day outside, but there's
no love in here.'
Robin Cook, to the Conservatives.

—WITTY AND WISE POLITICIANS—

'I cannot quite believe I am going to be 60. But I am escaping. I am going to Las Vegas and expect to spend the entire time in a drug-addled haze'
Edwina Currie, Former Conservative MP

'There is nothing so ex as an ex-MP.'
Tam Dalyell, Father of the House of Commons, on his retirement

'If I go for a walk through large parts of the south east, I am liable to be attacked and lynched.'
Alistair Darling, former Transport Secretary on the train network

'Am I happy? What do you take me for, an idiot?'
Charles De Gaulle, former French President

'Belgium is a country invented by the British to annoy the French.'
Charles De Gaulle

—WITTY AND WISE POLITICIANS—

'Talk to a man about himself and he will listen for hours.'

> *Benjamin Disraeli, 19th-Century*
> *British Prime Minister*

'Eight more days and I can start telling the truth again.'

> *Chris Dodd, Democrat Senator for Connecticut,*
> *on the Don Imus show, on campaigning*

'He gets so much in speaking fees these days that when I saw him in New York the other night and said hello to him he said, "That'll be $10".'

> *Bob Dole, US Senator on Bill Clinton*

'Like Marks and Spencer, we need both a good CEO and better frilly knickers.'

> *Alan Duncan, Tory MP, opens his campaign for*
> *the party leadership*

'There is nothing in Socialism that a little age or a little money will not cure.'

> *Will Durant, writer and philosopher*

—WITTY AND WISE POLITICIANS—

'In this world there are two kinds of people, my friend: those with loaded guns and those who dig. You dig.'

Clint Eastwood, actor, director and former Mayor of Carmel

'There's a whole range of things we're doing with condoms.'

Norman Fowler, former Conservative MP

'I hope you appreciate the fact that we decided to hold the mental health summit in the one building in London with the highest levels of anxiety, hysteria and paranoia we could find today.'

Liam Fox, Conservative MP, opening the event in the Palace of Westminster

"You know I love campaigning, but all I can think about is which art gallery I am going to visit when this is all over,"

Liam Fox

—WITTY AND WISE POLITICIANS—

"There's no point in asking focus groups. I go down the pub and hear about it there."

Liam Fox

'We must all hang together, or, assuredly, we shall all hang separately.'

Benjamin Franklin, US Statesman, at the signing of the Declaration of Independence

'There are few ironclad rules of diplomacy but to one there is an exception. When an official reports that talks were useful, it can safely be concluded that nothing was accomplished.'

J.K. Galbraith, US economist

'George W. Bush is flexible, friendly, open and a conservative – and in Washington there isn't a media computer that can write those four words in the same sentence.'

Newt Gingrich, former US House Speaker

—WITTY AND WISE POLITICIANS—

'People that are really very weird can get into sensitive positions and have tremendous impact on history.'

Al Gore, former US Vice-President

'The Conservative Establishment has always treated women as nannies, grannies and fannies.'

Teresa Gorman, former Conservative MP

'Cherie Blair's hairdressing costs for a trip to the USA were £2000. The most expensive haircut I ever had cost ten pounds: and nine pounds went on the search fee.'

William Hague, former Conservative leader

'It makes life very simple actually. You could be giving a TV interview in howling gale and it no longer matters.'

William Hague, on his bald head

'Grass doesn't grow on a busy street.'

William Hague, on his baldness

—WITTY AND WISE POLITICIANS—

'I did find it quite amusing to be lectured by lots of people in Fleet Street about having a beer too many. That was a bit ironic.'

William Hague, on his alleged 14 pints a day when a drayman

'I often think how much easier the world would have been to manage if Herr Hitler and Signor Mussolini had been to Oxford.'

Lord Halifax

'The Government needs a speedy and complete vasectomy.'

Neil Hamilton, disgraced former Conservative MP

'The attractive lady whom I had only recently been introduced to dropped into my lap ... I chose not to dump her off.'

Gary Hart, former Senator and Presidential candidate, on his encounter with model Donna Rice in 1988

—WITTY AND WISE POLITICIANS—

'England would win Euro 2000, Ilford would
demand independence from London and
Peter Mandelson would marry Joan Collins.'
>   *Lord Hattersley, on the truth according*
>   *to London cab drivers*

'Thanks to Railtrack, public ownership is
popular for the first time in 50 years.'
>   *Lord Hattersley*

'I was told it's exactly the same as the one
worn by Bill Clinton. It may not make your
hearing any better but it makes you irresistible
to 18-year-old girls.'
>   *Lord Hattersley, on his hearing aid*

'A Prime Minister who thinks it necessary to
explain how secure he is in office is really
admitting his tenure is coming to a rapid end'
>   *Lord Hattersley*

'The truth is that we English find hot weather
unnatural. To like it is to be unpatriotic.'
>   *Lord Hattersley*

—WITTY AND WISE POLITICIANS—

'Like David Brent, he's been sacked from his job but he's still hanging around.'
Oliver Heald, Conservative MP, commenting on John Prescott's lucky escape from a full cabinet sacking, having been allowed to retain the title while losing almost all responsibilities of the office of Deputy Prime Minister

'A statesman is a dead politician. I'm in the home of the living dead: the House of Lords.'
Lord Healey, Labour Peer

'Neutrality doesn't make sense – who are they neutral against?'
Lord Healey

'I tried to shave off my eyebrows once and my trousers fell down.'
Lord Healey

"Ocean racing is like standing under a cold shower tearing up £5 notes."
Edward Heath, former British Conservative Prime Minister

—WITTY AND WISE POLITICIANS—

'I have no interest in sailing around the world. Not that there is any lack of requests for me to do so.'

Edward Heath

'My mission is humanitarian. Therefore, it in no way represents the British Government.'

Edward Heath

'I keep telling my Tory colleagues: don't have any policies. A manifesto that has policies alienates people. In 1979 the manifesto said nothing which was brilliant.'

Lord Heseltine, Conservative peer

'One has to live with the ignominy of a garish sticker slapped over one's face, proclaiming £5, or more, off from the very beginning.'

Michael Heseltine, on the perils of selling his autobiography Life in the Jungle

'Fifty per cent of the public don't actually know what the term fifty per cent means.'

Patricia Hewitt, Secretary of State for Health

—WITTY AND WISE POLITICIANS—

'If ignorance goes to forty dollars a barrel, I want drilling rights to George Bush's head.'
> *Jim Hightower, former Texas Commissioner of Agriculture, referring to George Bush Senior*

'Chamberlain seemed such a nice old gentleman that I thought I would give him my autograph.'
> *Adolf Hitler, German Nazi dictator*

'Since I am no longer Sports Minister I have more time to be sporty.'
> *Kate Hoey, Labour MP*

'Blessed are the young, for they shall inherit the National Debt.'
> *Herbert Hoover, 31st US President*

'I regret to say that we of the FBI are powerless to act in cases of oral-genital intimacy, unless it has in some way obstructed interstate commerce.'
> *J. Edgar Hoover, former Director of the FBI*

—WITTY AND WISE POLITICIANS—

"There are now hardly any real people in the House of Commons."

Lord Howe,

'To err is human. To blame someone else is politics.'

Hubert H. Humphrey, former US Vice-President

'If I drink water I will have to go to the bathroom and how can I use the bathroom when my people are in bondage?'

Saddam Hussein, former President of Iraq, when offered a glass of water while in US custody.

'There is some truth in the media's claim that politicians are lying bastards.'

Sir Bernard Ingham, formerly Margaret Thatcher's press secretary

'I'm all for leaders who take a bit of time off. I used to say to Mrs Thatcher, "For heaven's sake! Let's have August off."'

Sir Bernard Ingham

—WITTY AND WISE POLITICIANS—

'She is physically not too bad, although she's shrunken with age and thin. She has very little short-term memory left. Still, it's always nice to see her.'

> *Sir Bernard Ingham, on Margaret Thatcher's well being*

"My money goes to my agent, then to my accountant and from him to the tax man."

> *Glenda Jackson, Labour MP*

"I used to believe that anything was better than nothing. Now I know that sometimes nothing is better."

> *Glenda Jackson*

'Acting is not very hard. The most important things are to be able to laugh and to cry.
If I have to cry, I think about my sex life. And if I have to laugh, well, I think of my sex life.'

> *Glenda Jackson*

—WITTY AND WISE POLITICIANS—

'I've found the future rather difficult to predict before it happens.'

> *Roy Jenkins, former Labour and SDP MP*

'The funkiest, most jiving party on earth.'

> *Boris Johnson, Conservative MP, on the*
> *Conservative Party*

'Have you ever struggled through one of Salman Rushdie's books to the end? Neither have I and neither, I bet, did the Ayatollah.'

> *Boris Johnson*

'I can hardly condemn UKIP as a bunch of boss-eyed, foam-flecked Euro hysterics, when I have been sometimes not far short of boss-eyed, foam-flecked hysteria myself.'

> *Boris Johnson, referring to the United Kingdom*
> *Independence Party*

'My chances of being PM are about as good as the chances of finding Elvis on Mars, or my being reincarnated as an olive.'

> *Boris Johnson*

—WITTY AND WISE POLITICIANS—

'The thing about sheep is that they are either alive or dead.'

Boris Johnson

'Your pratness is in fact the lubricant that makes your authority tolerable. Don't worry if you make a fool of yourself. Someone's got to. It's part of the job.'

Boris Johnson, on the role of bosses

'He has that special British cachet. He is the Hugh Grant of diplomacy.'

Boris Johnson, on Tony Blair

"To rely on a train in Blair's Britain is to engage in a crapshoot with the devil."

Boris Johnson

"Tremendous, little short of superb. On cracking form." [after being sacked of his role in the Tory shadow cabinet]

Boris Johnson

—WITTY AND WISE POLITICIANS—

"We pretend to be thick-skinned, we candidates, but there is one thing that makes us blush to the roots. What we hate, what we fear, is being ignored."

Boris Johnson

"For a second I am ashamed to say that I almost said no. I was overcome by a sudden attack of pomposity."

Tory Boris Johnson nearly turning down a newspaper offer of a car as he campaigned to defend his Henley constituency.

"I love tennis with a passion. I challenged Boris Becker to a match once and he said he was up for it but he never called back. I bet I could make him run around."

Boris Johnson

'Life isn't like coursework, baby. It's one damn essay crisis after another.'

Boris Johnson

—WITTY AND WISE POLITICIANS—

'The Conservative party conference is like a mixture between a Moonie wedding and the Jonestown massacre. But one hopes it will end more like the wedding than the massacre.'

Boris Johnson

"I could not fail to disagree with you less."

Boris Johnson, on 'Have I got News for You'

'I never trust a man unless I've got his pecker in my pocket.'

Lyndon B. Johnson, 36th US President

'All that Hubert needs over there is a gal to answer the phone and a pencil with an eraser on it.'

Lyndon B. Johnson, on Hubert Humphrey, his vice president.

'Making a speech on economics is a bit like pissing down your leg. It seems hot to you but never to anyone else.'

Lyndon B. Johnson

—WITTY AND WISE POLITICIANS—

'I want real loyalty. I want someone who will kiss my ass in Macy's window, and say it smells like roses.'

Lyndon B. Johnson

"Here in Devon we have to cope with people who come from as far afield as (cough) Somerset and even Wiltshire. I am having some difficulty living down the fact that I was born in Cornwall,"

Stanley Johnson, father of Boris, and Tory candidate for Teignbridge fielding reporters' questions regarding immigration

'Of the many things Greg Dyke might do, this is not one which is going to give me a sleepless night.'

Gerald Kaufman, Labour MP, on the proposal to move the BBC's Nine O'Clock News to 10pm

—WITTY AND WISE POLITICIANS—

"A clear conclusion has been reached, including by Conservatives, that the Conservatives are not going to win this election."
Charles Kennedy, former leader of the Liberal Democrats

"Not on your nelly."
Charles Kennedy speaking on BBC Radio 2's Jeremy Vine show when asked if he would form a coalition with a minority Labour government

'Forgive your enemies, but never forget their names.'
John F. Kennedy, 35th US President

'Let's face it, David Cameron is good eye candy.'
Oona King, former Labour MP

'There cannot be a crisis next week. My schedule is already full.'
Henry Kissinger, former US Politician

—WITTY AND WISE POLITICIANS—

'I don't read books, I write them.'

Henry Kissinger

'My first qualification for the great job of being Mayor of New York is my monumental personal ingratitude.'

Fiorello La Guardia, former Mayor of New York

'It is only when one begins to write things down that one sees the wisdom of not writing them down.'

Norman Lamont, former
Chancellor of the Exchequer

'Avoid popularity if you would have peace.'

Abraham Lincoln, 16th US President

'The lesson of history is that no one ever heeds the lessons of history.'

Lord Lipsey, Labour peer

—WITTY AND WISE POLITICIANS—

'Anybody who enjoys being in the House of Commons probably needs psychiatric help.'
Ken Livingstone, Mayor of London

'Many MPs never see the London that exists beyond the wine bars and brothels of Westminster.'

Ken Livingstone

'I'm too old to express an opinion on this.'
Nelson Mandela, former South African President, on David Beckham's hairstyle. The pair met in South Africa.

'When I am under the cosh and being pushed to my physical limit, I might suddenly reveal a fascinating piece of low-level gossip to distract him, or show intense interest in his life and welfare.'

Peter Mandelson, on his relationship with his personal trainer

—WITTY AND WISE POLITICIANS—

'I am always apprehensive about interrupting bingo. There can be howls of distress.'
Peter Mandelson, European Trade Commissioner and former Labour MP, on campaigning

'It's a badge of honour, but Clare Short has made me look like a loyalist.'
Bob Marshall-Andrews, named as the leading rebel Labour MP, referring to former Cabinet Minister Clare Short's rebellion against the War on Iraq

'I think that he got the message that separating a Scottish woman from her money is very difficult.'
Anne McGuire, Scottish Labour MP, after foiling a potential pickpocket in Portugal

'There are better ways to spend NHS money.'
Christine Mills, a Wolverhampton Conservative councillor, referring to a corset worth £250 – with false breasts and a belly bump – that has been bought so that young homeless men can experience being pregnant

—WITTY AND WISE POLITICIANS—

'The document is turgid, unreadable, stolid and legalistic. It has all the intellectual excitement of cold porridge.'

Austin Mitchell, Labour MP, on the European constitution

'I am not a Blair Babe. I'm a Blair Witch'

Margaret Moran, Labour MP

'We are not without accomplishment. We have managed to distribute poverty equally.'

Nguyen Co Thatch, former Vietnamese Foreign Minister

'It is no use pretending this is a molehill. It is Everest.'

Archie Norman, former Conservative MP and former Asda chairman, on the plight of his party

'At Oxford we drank to ludicrous and revolting excess and threw up over some of the most beautiful buildings in Britain.'

Steven Norris, former Conservative MP and London Mayoral Candidate

—WITTY AND WISE POLITICIANS—

'Flirting is a naughty pleasure and is infinitely preferable to using chat-up lines. Any man using a chat-up line shows he possesses complete intellectual aridity.'

Steven Norris

'In democracy everyone has the right to be represented, even the jerks.'

Chris Patten, last British Governor of Hong Kong

'I don't measure a man's success by how high he climbs but how high he bounces when he hits bottom.'

George S. Patton, former US General

'Working at Westminster is like having the nutters on the bus beside you every day.'

Amanda Platell, former Conservative Press Secretary

'Normally when I'm on holiday and I'm asked what I do, I say that I'm a traffic warden. That makes me much more popular.'

Steve Pound, Labour MP

—WITTY AND WISE POLITICIANS—

'All the Cabinet Ministers sat around the table with their heads nodding like cuckoo clocks.'
Enoch Powell, former Conservative MP

'During the election I met this chap who said, "You've got to help me, John. I've never had sex under a Labour government." If you're listening, mate, I hope the first hundred days were good for you!'
John Prescott, Deputy Prime Minister

'After 32 years in politics, swimming with sharks is a breeze.'
John Prescott, after swimming in a shark tank at an aquarium in Scotland

'Blair scares the life out of the Tories. And me.'
John Prescott

'The time has come to splatter the Tories!'
John Prescott

—WITTY AND WISE POLITICIANS—

'I am old Labour. I like kippers, not oysters.'
John Prescott, after his much-publicised visit to
Loch Fyne

'I'm meant to be the bloke who walks around
looking like he's going to club a baby seal.'
John Prescott, who says, since reports
of his new-found stepson, people have called
him a politician with a heart

'The right to suffer is one of the joys of a
free economy.'
Howard Pyle, aide to US President Dwight D.
Eisenhower, commenting on the unemployment
situation in Detroit

'Government is like a baby: a huge appetite
at one end and no sense of responsibility at
the other.'
Ronald Reagan, 40th US President

—WITTY AND WISE POLITICIANS—

'The most terrifying words in the English language are: I'm from the government and I'm here to help.'

Ronald Reagan

'Politics is not a bad profession. If you succeed there are many rewards. If you disgrace yourself you can always write a book.'

Ronald Reagan

'Recession is when a neighbour loses his job. Depression is when you lose yours.'

Ronald Reagan

'I have orders to be awakened at any time in the case of a national emergency, even if I'm in a cabinet meeting.'

Ronald Reagan

'I used to say that politics was the second lowest profession and I have come to know that it bears a great similarity to the first.'

Ronald Reagan

—WITTY AND WISE POLITICIANS—

'You can tell a lot about a fellow's character by his way of eating jellybeans.'

Ronald Reagan

'I never drink coffee at lunch. I find it keeps me awake for the afternoon.'

Ronald Reagan

'I can see a vacancy for him. There is one ancient British institution which is badly in need of such a coach. Five years ago it might have been the monarchy: now it is the Conservative Party.'

Lord Rees-Mogg, cross-bench peer, on Sven-Göran Eriksson, manager of the England football team

'Utter bollocks.'

John Reid, Defence Secretary, on an article by Roy Hattersley claiming that foundation hospitals will result in a two-tier health system

'I'm just an old maid with an attraction to men.'

Janet Reno, former US Attorney General, the first woman to hold the post

—WITTY AND WISE POLITICIANS—

'The future is not what it used to be.'
Sir Malcolm Rifkind, former Conservative MP

'The ablest man I ever met is the man you think you are.'
Franklin D. Roosevelt, 32nd US President

'When they call the roll in the Senate, the Senators do not know whether to answer "Present" or "Not guilty".'
Theodore Roosevelt, 26th US President

'A diplomat is somebody who can tell you to go to hell and leave you looking forward to the trip.'
Alex Salmond, former leader of the Scottish National Party

'I think it's about time we voted for senators with breasts. We've been voting for boobs long enough.'
Claire Sargent, Democrat Senate nominee

—WITTY AND WISE POLITICIANS—

'It's the most difficult [decision] I've made in my entire life, except the one I made in 1978 when I decided to get a bikini wax.'
Arnold Schwarzenegger, actor and Governor of California, announcing his gubernatorial candidacy on The Tonight Show With Jay Leno

'My old car manual is very useful but I don't read it much. I feel the same about the Labour manifesto.'
Mark Seddon, Editor of Tribune and Labour candidate for Buckingham

'The Army should take control of the Tory party.'
Dennis Skinner, Labour MP

'It's like shining a pencil torch into a dark void. There's a little bit of light coming through, but we need more work.'
Iain Duncan Smith, former Conservative Leader on trying to make Tories adopt the cause of social justice

—WITTY AND WISE POLITICIANS—

'We get criticised – and maybe not all the decisions we have made are right – but I don't see America as evil. We may be loud, but we are not assholes trying to take over the world.'

Jerry Springer, talk show host and ex-Mayor of Indianapolis, on his native America and the recent war in Iraq

'Clinton has kept all of the promises that he intended to keep.'

George Stephanopolous, on American chat show Larry King Live

'I'm having French lessons every week. And I can sing, "Ja, wir haben keinen Bananen", in German too.'

Jack Straw, leader of the Commons. The German translates to, "Yes, we have no bananas."

'It is to gays what Mein Kampf is to Jews.'

Peter Tatchell, homosexual rights campaigner, describing his least favourite book, the Bible

—WITTY AND WISE POLITICIANS—

'Gardens are like Marxist economies, full of five-year plans and objectives unattained but simply rolled over for another five years.'

Lord Tebbit, Conservative peer

'Europe is a place teeming with ill-intentioned persons.'

Margaret Thatcher, former British Conservative Prime Minister

'It is exciting to have a real crisis like the Falklands on your hands, when you have spent half your political life dealing with humdrum issues like the environment.'

Margaret Thatcher

'I don't mind how much my ministers talk: as long as they do what I say.'

Margaret Thatcher

'Economics are the method; the object is to change the soul.'

Margaret Thatcher

—WITTY AND WISE POLITICIANS—

'I always cheer up immensely if an attack is particularly wounding because I think, well, if they attack one personally, it means they have not a single political argument left.'

Margaret Thatcher

'Democratic nations must try to find ways to starve the terrorist and the hijacker of the oxygen of publicity on which they depend.'

Margaret Thatcher

'I am extraordinarily patient, provided I get my own way in the end.'

Margaret Thatcher

'You may have to fight a battle more than once to win.'

Margaret Thatcher

'The lady's not for turning.'

Margaret Thatcher

—WITTY AND WISE POLITICIANS—

'Being Prime Minister is a lonely job ... you cannot lead from the crowd.'

Margaret Thatcher

'I don't know what I would do without Whitelaw. Everyone should have a Willy.'

Margaret Thatcher

'As God once said, and I think rightly ...'

Margaret Thatcher

'I have very strong views about Europe. We're quite the best country. We rescued them. We're not going to get entangled with them. We've got to keep our own independence. Is that clear?'

Margaret Thatcher

'Being powerful is like being a lady. If you have to tell people you are, you aren't.'

Margaret Thatcher

'Always be sincere, even if you don't mean it.'

Harry S. Truman, 33rd US President

—WITTY AND WISE POLITICIANS—

'It is amazing what you can accomplish if you do not care who gets the credit.'

Harry S. Truman

'At the age of 81, I am left with one pleasure and that's passive smoking. I love it.'

Baroness Trumpington, Conservative peer

'People have forgotten the effects of prohibition. We have become the United States of Amnesia.'

Gore Vidal, writer

'The beautiful city of Edinburgh is the most drug-infested place in Europe. Another triumph for the American way.'

Gore Vidal

'When you say you agree to a thing in principle you mean that you have not the slightest intention of carrying it out in practice.'

Otto Von Bismarck, former German Chancellor

—WITTY AND WISE POLITICIANS—

'Never believe anything in politics until it has been officially denied.'

Otto Von Bismarck

'The first time I wore a trouser suit to the Commons, Nicholas Soames asked me why I was wearing my pyjamas.'

*Baroness Walmsley, Liberal
Democrat peer*

'Few men have virtue to withstand the highest bidder.'

George Washington, 1st US President

'John Prescott had been to Hull and back.'

*Roland Watson, chief political
correspondent, The Times*

—WITTY AND WISE POLITICIANS—

'When I asked her last week what she planned to do after the general election defeat she just hit me.'
Charlie Whelan, former New Labour spin doctor, referring to a conversation with Amanda Platell, the Conservative chief press officer, prior to the 2001 General Election

'I'd want the press to be there because they would have to be polite.'
Ann Widdecombe, Conservative MP, on her own funeral

'People talk to me more slowly now.' [on being blonde]
Ann Widdecombe

'People who look perfectly normal and are obviously healthy are worrying themselves into a passion because they put on half a stone over Christmas. Anyone would think that St Peter stands at the Pearly Gates with a tape measure.'
Ann Widdecombe

—WITTY AND WISE POLITICIANS—

'Women are so wet. They moan that men are rude to them, but then men are just as rude to men.'

Ann Widdecombe

'I am finally giving the electorate what they have always wanted. They will be seeing less of me.'

Ann Widdecombe, regarding her weight-loss

'My cat did that the other day when he came in from the garden.'

Ann Widdecombe, on the New Labour logo

'I have not a single vandalistic bone in my body, but the sight of Oliver Cromwell's statue outside the House of Commons causes me a quick grinding of the teeth. He was a bigot, a regicide and a deeply oppressive ruler.'

Ann Widdecombe

—WITTY AND WISE POLITICIANS—

'I was walking across King's Cross station when a drunken Irishman came stumbling up and flung his arms around me. He wanted to thank me for the peace process in Northern Ireland.'
Ann Widdecombe, on being mistaken for Mo Mowlam

'Politics is full of people who conspire against you, lie, distort what you have said and seek your downfall.'
Ann Widdecombe

'I haven't got a butler. We just have three people who look after the house. End of story.'
Shaun Woodward, Labour MP

'Why do we have endless debates about whether to kill foxes, but no debate on whether to kill people?'
Tony Wright, Chair of the Public Administration Select Committee, on whether MPs would have the chance to vote on going to war in Iraq

—WITTY AND WISE POLITICIANS—

'No country which has cricket as one of its national games has yet gone Communist.'
Woodrow Wyatt, former Conservative MP

'From now on, somebody else is responsible for the nuclear button. Maybe it will be easier to beat insomnia now?'
Boris Yeltsin, former Russian President,
on his feelings having retired from the
Russian Presidency

8

WIT ABOUT
POLITICS

—— WIT ABOUT POLITICS ——

'Growing older, I have lost the need to be political, which means, in this country, the need to be left. I am driven into grudging toleration of the Conservative Party because it is the party of non-politics, of resistance to politics.'
Kingsley Amis, novelist and poet

'I am to the Fringe what Ann Widdecombe is to designer drugs.'
Clive Anderson, talk-show host, on the Edinburgh Festival

'Pro is to con as progress is to congress.'
Anon

'It was like kissing a can opener.'
Godfrey Barker, art expert, on kissing Edwina Currie when they were both students at Oxford

'He has about as much charisma as a pair of dentures grinning in a glass of water.'
Trevor Bayliss, the clockwork radio inventor, on Tony Blair

—— WIT ABOUT POLITICS ——

'A government that robs Peter to pay Paul can always depend on the support of Paul.'
George Bernard Shaw, dramatist

"I know he is not pretty, but it has nothing to do with what you look like,"
Honor Blackman, former Bond girl, on Charles Kennedy, whom she supported

'I wouldn't want to move to a smaller house.'
Bono, on why he would never run for US President

'One way to avoid war is to give Bush and Saddam a toddler each to look after with no help.'
Rory Bremner, comedian and impressionist

'Some mornings I wake and think, Shall I study this Stephen Byers tape or shall I get a life?
Rory Bremner, referring to the former Labour minister

────── WIT ABOUT POLITICS ──────

'Iain Duncan Smith has the potential to be one of the great comic characters in politics.'

Rory Bremner, on IDS before his fall

"Like a fish, New Labour is rotting from the head down,"

Rory Bremner

'Lucky it's Blair's toenails Cherie collects, not fingernails. How else can he cling to power?'

Rory Bremner

He's a salesman. He sells dreams. He could sell sand to the Arabs.'

Rory Bremner on Tony Blair

'George was a great one for whoopee cushions when he was a drinking man. But I'd be surprised if he was into that sort of thing any more.'

Billy Bush, reporter and President Bush's cousin

———— WIT ABOUT POLITICS ————

"He does have a face that only a lesbian could love,"
Julie Burchill, columnist, on former Leader of the Liberal Democrats Charles Kennedy

'Democracy is being allowed to vote for the candidate you dislike least.'
Robert Byrne, author, cartoonist, journalist and philosopher

'You can get much further with a kind word and a gun than you can with a kind word alone.'
Al Capone, gangster

'If life were fair, Dan Quayle would be making a living asking, Do you want fries with that?
John Cleese, comedian and actor

'Most of what you read in the papers is lies. And I should know, because a lot of the lies you see in the papers are mine.'
Max Clifford, publicist

——— WIT ABOUT POLITICS ———

'The gradual, soul-destroying realisation that
you have been most monumentally had ... the
revolution is not only not televised, it is not
going to occur at all.'
Jarvis Cocker, musician, on his disillusionment
with the Labour Party

'He's like an actor who doesn't really believe in
his script himself but has the incredible skill to
make everyone else believe in it.'
Tom Conti, actor, on Tony Blair

'Nixon's motto was: If two wrongs don't make a
right, try three.'
Norman Cousins, editor and writer

'I don't believe in anti-capitalism. Democracy is
built on inequality and I'd rather be in a
democracy than a fat-cat communist regime.'
Jason Donovan, actor and singer

──────── WIT ABOUT POLITICS ────────

'There is a simple and practical method of putting this long-suffering government out of its misery. Since sex scandals seem to be the only method of dislodging a politician from his post, it is the duty of every patriotic woman to bear a love child by a Tory MP.'

Mararette Driscoll, journalist

'I still find being slagged off by some second-rate backbench MP a pain in the arse.'

Greg Dyke, former Director General of the BBC

'Young people are very, very interested in the way the world is run – everything from education to the NHS – but there is not anyone in the Cabinet that can relate to me or that I can relate to.'

Ms Dynamite, singer and rap artist

'It is a slightly different tactic, but it has kept people away.'

Harry Enfield, comedian, explaining why he has put up a giant poster of Harold Wilson in his front window

———— WIT ABOUT POLITICS ————

'Kerry said "more leaders", not "foreign
leaders". In other news, Bush said, "My mom
does crunches for ab reduction", not "Saddam
has weapons of mass destruction."'

www.Fark.com

'Cronyism is a word recently invented by the
Tories so that they can attack Labour for doing
what Tories have done since time immemorial.'

Paul Foot, political commentator

'My eye was caught by an article for a new
hearing aid "that lets you hear only what you
want". Nothing revolutionary there. Politicians
have been wearing them for years.'

Frederick Forsyth, novelist

'I'll eat a large brown envelope if they find a
hollowed-out mountain full of uranium.'

*Frederick Forsyth, on the prospects of finding
weapons of mass destruction in Iraq*

——————— WIT ABOUT POLITICS ———————

"I think it's a very good year for abstention,"
*Stephen Fry, actor and writer, on the last
election. He is normally a Labour supporter*

'Politics is the art of choosing between the
disastrous and the unpalatable.'
John Galbraith, economist

'Bono wants to change the world by embracing
it. I get angry and want to punch its lights out.
We are the Laurel and Hardy of international
politics.'
Bob Geldof

'I'm from a little place called England – we
used to run the world before you.'
*Ricky Gervais, comedian, referring to America
during his acceptance speech after winning two
Golden Globes for* The Office

——— WIT ABOUT POLITICS ———

'I don't know a lot about politics but I have great trust in him as a leader'

> *Geri Halliwell, former Spice Girl,*
> *on why she was appearing in an*
> *election broadcast for Tony Blair*

'Never underestimate the hypocrisy of politicians.'

> *James Herbert, novelist*

'We'd all like to vote for the best man but he's never a candidate.'

> *Kin Hubbard, cartoonist, journalist*
> *and philosopher*

'I'm convinced Gordon Brown bores 99 per cent of any audience. I once interviewed him for 38 minutes and he gave the same answer to every question. And he doesn't care that everyone finds him so boring.'

> *John Humphrys, presenter of*
> *BBC Radio 4's Today*

———— WIT ABOUT POLITICS ————

'That was insignificant to me. It was just a continuation of what was going on in the world. The Americans have started this nonsensical term "war on terrorism". Well, excuse me, but it's the Yanks who have been funding the IRA for the last 30 years.'

Chrissie Hynde, singer, on 11th September terrorist attacks

'The British Secret Service was staffed at one point almost entirely by alcoholic homosexuals working for the KGB.'

Clive James, writer and broadcaster

'I'm travelling in Spain where everyone's using the euro. They haven't all drowned; everyone's speaking Spanish; they haven't become English, they haven't become Welsh, they haven't become Afghans.'

Eddie Izzard, comedian and actor, on an anti-euro campaign that was backed by some celebrities

———— WIT ABOUT POLITICS ————

'As a topic, weapons of mass destruction is nuclear, or at the very least, "nucular".'

Mark Katz, ex-Clinton joke writer,
on Bush's WMD

'He has made just one trip to Europe, spends four minutes determining whether someone should be put to death, and his environmental policies are not only shameful, they should be criminal.'

Jessica Lange, actress, on George W. Bush

'Apart from that, Mrs Lincoln, how did you enjoy the play?'

Tom Lehrer, musician and comedian

'Politics is show business for ugly people. The women aren't as attractive. The men aren't as handsome. The money is not as good. Being in politics is basically like being in B movies.'

Jay Leno, US talk show host

—————— WIT ABOUT POLITICS ——————

'You felt you didn't have to attend meetings, just give them your Visa number.'

Ken Loach, film director,
on why he left the Labour Party

'In Victorian and Edwardian times, the cleverest people went into politics. Now they go to Goldman Sachs.'

Kelvin MacKenzie, former editor of the Sun,
bemoaning the quality of MPs

'Since when is offensive language a reason for being unpopular? I find the language of George W. Bush much more offensive.'

Madonna, singer, on rap artist Eminem

'Conservatives are people who look at a tree and feel instinctively that it is more beautiful than anything they can name. But when it comes to defending that tree against a highway, they will go for the highway.'

Norman Mailer, writer and journalist

—— WIT ABOUT POLITICS ——

"What strikes me is how incredibly useless the political classes actually are at assessing the state of the nation."
Andrew Marr, the BBC's political editor

'One aspect of politics too little acknowledged is that besides being jolly serious and all that, it is also a hugely enjoyable game for boys.'
Andrew Marr

'When politicians call for "quiet reflection", you know something has happened for which they didn't have a speech ready.'
Andrew Marr on the French referendum

'Politics is the art of looking for trouble, finding it everywhere, diagnosing it incorrectly, and applying the wrong remedies.'
Groucho Marx, comedian and actor

'A good politician is quite as unthinkable as an honest burglar.'
H.L. Mencken, newspaperman, book reviewer, and political commentator

──────── WIT ABOUT POLITICS ────────

'Edwina Curry is the female Margaret Thatcher.'
Mrs Merton (Caroline Quentin,
writer and comedienne)

'A smaller majority concentrates the mind.'
Alan Milburn

'The only way the French are going in is if we
tell them we found truffles in Iraq.'
Dennis Miller, US comedien, on France's refusal
to back the war in Iraq, in 2003

'I would like to apologise for referring to
George W. Bush as a "deserter". What I meant
to say is that George W. Bush is a deserter, an
election thief, a drunk driver, a WMD liar and a
functional illiterate. And he poops his pants.'
Michael Moore, satirist and film-maker

—— WIT ABOUT POLITICS ——

'We're too lazy to get out of bed. This is our problem. Conservatives are up at, like, six in the morning. They're up to greet the sunrise and screw the poor. They're kicking ass and taking names by the time we're still looking for a cappuccino.'

Michael Moore, on Democrats in the USA

'Prime Minister's children are not in the job description.'

Andrew Motion, former Poet Laureate, on whether he is going to write a poem to celebrate the birth of the Blair baby

'The problem with New Labour is that they drink too much coffee, so they are always thinking up stupid ideas. Ordinary people have got a pint in hand and not a thought in their heads, and that's the way it should be.'

Al Murray, comedian

'Any political party that includes the word "democratic" in its name isn't.'

Patrick Murray, author

——— WIT ABOUT POLITICS ———

'The enemy isn't conservatism. The enemy isn't liberalism. The enemy is bullshit.'

Lars-Erik Nelson, journalist

'Politicians are interested in people. Not that this is always a virtue. Fleas are interested in dogs.'

P.J. O'Rourke, author and satirist

'The Democrats are the party of government activism, the party that says government can make you richer, smarter, taller, and get the chickweed out of your lawn. Republicans are the party that says government doesn't work, and then get elected and prove it.'

P.J. O'Rourke

'Politicians are wonderful people as long as they stay away from things they don't understand, such as working for a living.'

P.J. O'Rourke

——— WIT ABOUT POLITICS ———

'If he's born here, the only problem is that he can never be President of the United States.'

Gwyneth Paltrow, actress, considering the downside of her child being born in the United Kingdom

'News from Westminster is that there is to be no Nativity tableau this year. It's not for religious reasons, just that they can't find three wise men and a virgin. There is no problem, however, in finding enough asses to fill the stable.'

Jeremy Paxman, broadcaster and presenter of BBC2's Newsnight

'The life of a mule harnessed to a wheel can have more excitement in it than that of a Government backbencher in our Parliament.'

Jeremy Paxman

'Internationally, football has become a substitute for war.'

Jeremy Paxman

———— WIT ABOUT POLITICS ————

'One of the penalties for refusing to participate in politics is that you end up being governed by your inferiors.'

Plato, philosopher

'Politicians are people who, when they see the light at the end of the tunnel, go out and buy some more tunnel.'

John Quinton, Metropolitan Police
Committee chairman

'The draft is white people sending black people to fight yellow people to protect the country they stole from red people.'

James Rado, musician

'Democracy is too good to share with just anybody.'

Nigel Rees, writer and broadcaster

———— WIT ABOUT POLITICS ————

'Americans are quite poor on literature and politics – and they do not know anywhere outside Idaho.'
Anne Robinson, TV presenter/game show host, on US contestants on The Weakest Link

'The Tories' main problem is that they don't have anyone you'd want to go to bed with.'
Anne Robinson

'To hell with George Bush. God save America.'
Anita Roddick, founder of The Body Shop

'Congress is so strange. A man gets up to speak and says nothing. Nobody listens. Then everybody disagrees with him.'
Will Rogers, American humorist, performer and journalist

'Stupidity got us here: it can get us out.'
Will Rogers

———— WIT ABOUT POLITICS ————

'A fool and his money are soon elected.'
Will Rogers

'I don't make jokes. I just watch the government and report the facts.'
Will Rogers

'I do not belong to any organised political party: I'm a democrat.'
Will Rogers

'It's easy being a humorist when you've got the whole government working for you.'
Will Rogers

"I haven't had the full stats done yet but Welsh rugby does seem to get more Grand Slams when we have Labour governments,"
Mike Ruddock, Wales rugby coach

────── WIT ABOUT POLITICS ──────

'These people like Ben Elton suddenly criticising New Labour. It's the first ever recorded case of rats leaving a floating ship.'
Alexei Sayle, comedian and writer

'Americans have different ways of saying things. They say "elevator", we say "lift"; they say "President", we say "stupid psychopathic git".'
Alexei Sayle

'I didn't live through 300 years of Tory rule to live through another 300 years of Tory rule in a nicer suit.'
Alexei Sayle, criticising the Blair Government

'When she reads out the Ten Commandments at Westminster Cathedral it sounds as though she has written them herself.'
Father Michael Seed, on Ann Widdecombe

———— WIT ABOUT POLITICS ————

'You've done a nice job decorating the
White House.'

> *Jessica Simpson, pop star, on being
> introduced to Interior Secretary Gale Norton
> while touring the White House*

'Why is there news? Why do they have it? It's so
depressing.'

> *Anna Nicole Smith, former Playboy model*

'The House of Commons is the longest-running
farce in the West End.'

> *Cyril Smith, former Liberal MP*

'Presentationally, Bill Clinton is a US President
to die for. The truth is, far too many have.'

> *Jon Snow, newsreader on Channel 4*

'Tony Blair? I've never heard of him.'

> *Britney Spears, pop singer*

——— WIT ABOUT POLITICS ———

'I don't think he's stupid. I think we're stupid, because, if we weren't, he wouldn't talk to us this way.'

Jon Stewart, TV host, on President George W. Bush

It's important to take them seriously – most people don't.'

Ben Summerskill, Chief Executive of gay rights lobby group, Stonewall, on politicians

'Whether you are an ex-politician or an ex-spouse or whatever, there comes a time when you have to say, "I've had my innings. Pipe down." That's my daughterly advice.'

Carol Thatcher, journalist, on her mother, Margaret

'Ninety-eight per cent of the adults in this country are decent, hard-working, honest Americans. It's the other lousy two per cent that get all the publicity. But then – we elected them.'

Lily Tomlin, comedienne and actor

————— WIT ABOUT POLITICS —————

"At the age of 81, I am left with one pleasure and that's passive smoking. I love it."

Baroness Trumpington

'When the missionaries came to Africa, they had the Bible and we had the land. They said, "Let us pray." We closed our eyes. When we opened them, we had the Bible and they had the land.'

Archbishop Desmond Tutu,
South African priest and politician

'Suppose you were an idiot, and suppose you were a member of congress; but I repeat myself.'

Mark Twain, writer

'I never became a politician because I could not stand the strain of being right all the time.'

Peter Ustinov, actor, writer and director

'Politics is the art of preventing people from taking part in affairs that properly concern them.'

Paul Valery, poet, critic and thinker

——— WIT ABOUT POLITICS ———

'They say he's dyslexic, but he's not. He just has a real problem speaking.'

Robert Vaughan, actor, on George W. Bush

'An ideal form of government is democracy tempered with assassination.'

Voltaire

'It is not only saloon-bar chest-prodders who are now asking how we propose to get a war on Iraq together when we can't even de-ice the M11.'

Keith Waterhouse, columnist and playwright

'The only remaining question, as we are sucked into the European currency as remorselessly as bathwater down a plughole, is whether we will be bullied, bamboozeld, blackmailed, bludgeoned, badgered or simply bored into accepting the euro.'

Keith Waterhouse

—————— WIT ABOUT POLITICS ——————

'I couldn't possibly vote Conservative while William Hague still leads the party. There is nothing personal in this, it's purely on class grounds.'
Auberon Waugh, writer, journalist and satirist

'Democracy means simply the bludgeoning of the people by the people for the people.'
Oscar Wilde, writer

'You'll notice that Nancy Reagan never drinks water when Ronnie speaks.'
Robin Williams, actor and comedian

'I don't care about Cherie Blair and about Tony Blair. I don't care about them people. At the end of the day, to get from A to Z they lose their morals.'
Ray Winstone, actor

9

OFFENSIVE POLITICIANS

——OFFENSIVE POLITICIANS——

'Once you've seen one ghetto, you've seen them all.'

Spiro T. Agnew, former Governor of Maryland and Nixon's Vice-President

"If you find an Australian indoors, it's a fair bet that he will have a glass in his hand."

Jonathan Aitken, disgraced former Conservative MP, who was jailed for perjury

'I was elected by a bunch of fat, stupid, ugly old ladies that watch soap operas, play bingo, read tabloids and don't know the metric system.'

Tom Alciere, former US Republican in the House of Representatives

'You can achieve more, can get more, but because of your little minds you cannot get what you are expected to get.'

Daniel Arap Moi, former President of Kenya, addressing a Nairobi womens' seminar in 2001

———— OFFENSIVE POLITICIANS ————

'I have a prejudice against drunk women that I don't have against drunk men, because it's so unnatural for them to behave like that.'

Martin Bell, former Independent MP

'We have a saying: "The dogs bark but the caravan continues." People can bark and it will not bother us. Why should it?'

The Shah of Iran, in the 1970s

'An AIDS patient asks his doctor whether the sand treatment prescribed him will do any good. "No," the doctor replies, "but you will get accustomed to living under the earth."'

Silvio Berlusconi, former Italian Prime Minister

'Those judges are doubly mad! In the first place, because they are politically mad, and in the second place because they are mad anyway. If they do that job it is because they are anthropologically different from the rest of the human race.'

Silvio Berlusconi, on judges pursuing former prime minister Giulio Andreotti on charges relating to the Mafia

———— OFFENSIVE POLITICIANS ————

'They have lost their minds; they really have
come to the end of the line, indeed they have
gone beyond it. I would advise them, too, to
undergo sand treatment...'

*Silvio Berlusconi, in response to critics who
found the joke offensive*

'Italy is a great country to invest in these days.
The proof is that the Italian Prime Minister
has invested all his money there ... Another
reason to invest in Italy is that today we have
fewer communists. There were 34 per cent of
them when I entered politics ten years ago.
Today there are only 16 per cent ... Another
reason to invest in Italy is that we have
beautiful secretaries.'

Silvio Berlusconi

'Parma is synonymous with good cuisine. The
Finns don't even know what prosciutto is. I
cannot accept this.'

*Silvio Berlusconi, on a proposal to base an EU
food standards agency in Finland, rather than the
Italian city of Parma*

——OFFENSIVE POLITICIANS——

'No small businessman with a brain would ever employ a lady of child-bearing age.'
> *Godfrey Bloom, UKIP's MEP for Yorkshire and the Humber*

'That is so 1950s. It seems Senator Edwards lacks disability etiquette.'
> *Debbie Bonomo, wheelchair user, after White House Democrat hopeful John Edwards patted her head during campaigning*

'You know, you might have benefited from that. No? Gee, it's time! Because you're a nice girl, you know.'
> *Jean Chretien, former Canadian Prime Minister, advising a female reporter to become pregnant to take advantage of generous maternity benefits*

'I don't know if I am in West, South, North or East Jerusalem right now.'
> *Jean Chretien*

'Bongo Bongo Land'
> *Alan Clark, former Conservative MP, on Africa*

—— OFFENSIVE POLITICIANS ——

'Good Christian people will not get AIDS.'
Edwina Currie, writer, broadcaster and former
Conservative politician

'People in the north die of ignorance
and crisps.'
Edwina Currie

'Buy long johns, check your hot-water bottles,
knit gloves and scarves and get your
grandchildren to give you a woolly nightcap.'
Edwina Currie, giving advice to pensioners on
how to keep warm during the winter

'Yes, it's the politics of envy. We're envious of
company directors' wealth. These people are
stinking lousy thieving incompetent scum.'
Frank Dobson, Labour MP

——— OFFENSIVE POLITICIANS ———

'I'm sick and tired of strong women pretending that they can't cope with a "masculine" working environment. If they can't deal with it they should go back home and do some knitting.'

Gwyneth Dunwoody, Labour MP,
on House of Commons reform

'All this notion of gollies being derogatory to black people is nonsense.'

Richard Eddy, former Deputy
Leader of the Tory Group

'I was an expert on migration problems.'

Adolf Eichmann, Nazi war criminal and
head of the Austrian office for Jewish
immigration during WWII

'What is a skirt but an open gateway?'
Sir Nicholas Fairbairn, former conservative MP

——— OFFENSIVE POLITICIANS ———

'If combat means living in a ditch, females have
biological problems staying in a ditch for 30
days because they get infections and they don't
have upper body strength. I mean, some do,
but they're relatively rare. On the other hand,
men are basically little piglets, you drop them
in the ditch, they roll around in it, doesn't
matter, you know. These things are very real.
On the other hand, if combat means being on
an Aegis-class cruiser managing the computer
controls for twelve ships and their rockets, a
female may be again dramatically better than a
male who gets very, very frustrated sitting in a
chair all the time because males are biologically
driven to go out and hunt giraffes.'

*Newt Gingrich, former Speaker, US House of
Representatives*

'Members of Parliament are, on the whole,
quicker and more articulate than ordinary
mortals.'

Sir Archie Hamilton, former Conservative MP

OFFENSIVE POLITICIANS

'I hope I don't sound patronising, but it's more difficult for women to take the rational approach that I do, because of the emotional cycle that follows a woman's physical cycle.'
Neil Hamilton, disgraced former Conservative MP

'People who watch morning television are elderly, infirm or emotionally immature.'
Lord Hattersley, Labour peer

'Apart from oil - which was discovered, is produced and is paid for by the west - what do they contribute? Can you think of anything? Anything really useful? Anything really valuable? Something we really need, could not do without? No, nor can I.'
Robert Kilroy-Silk, ex-TV presenter and now leader of Veritas, talking about the Middle East

'He was 'doing it in the name of Islam' [Kilroy's claim on a man who poured slurry over him]
Robert Kilroy-Silk

———— OFFENSIVE POLITICIANS ————

'Poorer people don't have cars.'
Ken Livingstone, Mayor of London

'One thing that Chairman Mao did was to end the appalling foot binding of women. That alone justifies the Mao Tse-tung era.'
Ken Livingstone

'Most beggars are Scottish and I've never met one yet who politely and gently asked for money. There are no genuine beggars. Those who are in need have got all the social benefits they require. Beggars are doing so out of choice because they find it more pleasant. I always give them something – I give them a piece of my mind.'
David Maclean, Conservative MP

———— OFFENSIVE POLITICIANS ————

'Memorial services are the cocktail parties of the geriatric set.'

> *Harold Macmillan, former British*
> *Conservative Prime Minister*

'Of course we are not patronising women. We are just going to explain to them in words of one syllable what it is all about.'

> *Lady Olga Maitland, former Conservative MP*

'Mussolini's ideas were 99 per cent good, and 1 per cent maybe questionable.'

> *Guido Mussolini, Benito Mussolini's grandson*
> *and candidate for Mayor of Rome*

'Marijuana smokers, drug addicts, long-hairs, homosexuals and unionists.'

> *Augusto Pinochet, former President of Chile, on*
> *the West German Army*

—— OFFENSIVE POLITICIANS ——

'I don't like fancy food. It's difficult in China because you don't know what's in the bloody dish.'

John Prescott, Deputy Prime Minister.
His culinary preferences risked whipping
up a diplomatic storm

'When the French are building their affordable homes, then it is bound to cost more, because they've got to put in all those bloody bidets.'

John Prescott

'Rural Americans are real Americans. You can't always be sure with other Americans. Not all of them are real.'

Dan Quayle, former US Vice-President

'Feminism encourages women to leave their husbands, kill their children, practise witchcraft, destroy capitalism and become lesbians.'

Reverend Pat Robertson, at the 1992 'Grand Old
Party' – a republican convention

——— OFFENSIVE POLITICIANS ———

'I saw this toilet bowl. How many times do you get away with this – to take a woman, grab her upside down, and bury her face in a toilet bowl? I wanted to have something floating there ... The thing is, you can do it, because, in the end, I didn't do it to a woman – she's a machine! We could get away with it without being crucified by who-knows-what group.'

Arnold Schwarzenegger, actor and governor of California, describing a scene in Terminator 3

'As much as when you see a blonde with great tits and a great ass, you say to yourself, "Hey, she must be stupid or must have nothing else to offer," which maybe is the case many times. But then again there is the one that is as smart as her breasts look, great as her face looks, beautiful as her whole body looks gorgeous, you know, so people are shocked.'

Arnold Schwarzenegger, in an interview with Esquire

——— OFFENSIVE POLITICIANS ———

'I can look at a chick who's a little out of shape and, if she turns me on, I won't hesitate to date her. If she's a good f**k she can weigh 150 pounds, I don't care.'

Arnold Schwarzenegger, in a 1977
interview with Oui

'All these black people are screwing up my democracy.'

Ian Smith, PM of former Rhodesia,
now Zimbabwe

'Every kind of mix you can have. I have a black, I have a woman, two Jews and a cripple.'

James Watt, US Interior Secretary, describing the
members of a commission he set up, in 1983.
Soon afterwards, he was removed from the job

10

POLITICIANS ON THEMSELVES

—POLITICIANS ON THEMSELVES—

'Fun-loving guy seeks peace.'
Gerry Adams, President of Sinn Fein, when asked
his lonely hearts advertisement would read

'I don't use dye at all. However, I do use one of
those shampoos that helps make your hair
sparkle.'
Jonathan Aitken, disgraced former Conservative
MP, on his grooming habits

'I am a great mayor; I am an upstanding
Christian man; I am an intelligent man; I am a
deeply educated man; I am a humble man.'
Marion Barry, former Mayor of
Washington, D.C.

'I enjoy all the privileges of being a peer
without the humiliation of actually being one.'
Tony Benn, Former Labour MP, who is allowed to
sit in the peers gallery of the House of Commons

'The right man in the right job.'
Silvio Berlusconi, former Italian Prime Minister

—POLITICIANS ON THEMSELVES—

'Out of love for Italy, I felt I had to save it from
the left.'

*Silvio Berlusconi, former Italian
Prime Minister on himself*

'The best political leader in Europe and in
the world.'

Silvio Berlusconi

'There is noone on the world stage who can
compete with me.'

Silvio Berlusconi

'I don't need to go into office for the power. I
have houses all over the world, stupendous
boats ... beautiful airplanes, a beautiful wife, a
beautiful family ... I am making a sacrifice.'

Silvio Berlusconi

'I look in the mirror and I like what I see and I
think I am more pleasing to others too.'

Silvio Berlusconi, on his recent plastic surgery

— POLITICIANS ON THEMSELVES —

'I can only go one way. I haven't got a
reverse gear.'

Tony Blair, British Prime Minister

"I'm not saying there haven't been tensions.
It passes."
Tony Blair, on his relationship with Gordon Brown

'The illness has given me time to think – which
is always dangerous.'

*David Blunkett, former Home Secretary,
recovering from surgery on his digestive system*

'I can hear people smile.'

David Blunkett

'I'm also not very analytical. You know I don't
spend a lot of time thinking about myself,
about why I do things.'

George W. Bush, US President

'I'm the master of low expectations.'

George W. Bush

—POLITICIANS ON THEMSELVES—

'This is what I'm good at. I like meeting people, my fellow citizens, I like interfacing with them.'

George W. Bush

'God loves you, and I love you. And you can count on both of us as a powerful message that people who wonder about their future can hear.'

George W. Bush

'I glance at the headlines just to kind of get a flavour for what's moving. I rarely read the stories, and get briefed by people who have probably read the news themselves.'

George W. Bush

'I know something about being a government. And you've got a good one.'

George W. Bush

'I am not one who – who flamboyantly believes in throwing a lot of words around.'

George Bush, Sr, 41st US President

— POLITICIANS ON THEMSELVES —

'Some days I wonder if I'll ever do anything
meaningful and worthwhile again.'

Alastair Campbell

'No one ever believes this, but I didn't go into
politics to be Prime Minister.'

*David Cameron, leader of the Conservative
Party, on Channel 4's Richard and Judy*

'I can't wait for the next series of Desperate
Housewives.'

*David Cameron at the National
Television Awards*

'You know me. I like a good fight. I'm a bit
anxious to have a fight.'

*Jean Chretien, former Canadian Prime Minister,
on why he called an election*

'Although I am prepared for martyrdom, I was
willing to have it postponed.'

*Winston Churchill, former
British Prime Minister*

—POLITICIANS ON THEMSELVES—

'It makes one want to despair.'
>*Winston Churchill, grandson of the Winston Churchill, on hearing many teenagers think his grandfather was an insurance salesman*

'I don't have a beer belly. It's a Burgundy belly and it cost me a lot of money.'
>*Charles Clarke, former Home Secretary*

'I am killing myself because I want it done. Hard enough to live my life the first time. The second time has really been tough.'
>*Bill Clinton, 42nd US President, on writing his memoirs*

'I have been described as fat, dishevelled, disgusting, balding and an utter disgrace. But I have had a bad press as well.'
>*Lord Falconer, the Lord Chancellor*

"Drunkenness, bad manners, bigotry and ignorance" [pet hates]
>*George Galloway, former Labour MP and leader of Respect*

—POLITICIANS ON THEMSELVES—

'I'm not a politician of your ordinary type. Most politicians - and most politics - are boring.... I don't think I am boring.'

George Galloway

'They say that politics is show business for ugly people, but as I always crack, what would I know about that? I like a challenge.'

George Galloway

'I am Al Gore, and I used to be the next President of the United States of America.'

Al Gore, former US Vice-President

'It is probably exaggerated, the extent to which I was loathed.'

Michael Howard, former Conservative leader, on his time as Home Secretary

'Look, I am a lawyer, I know about giving advice,'

Michael Howard, former Conservative leader, talking about Lord Goldsmith's change in advice on the war

—POLITICIANS ON THEMSELVES—

'If I'm too strong for some people, that's their problem.'

Glenda Jackson, Labour MP

'If I did try to acquire gravitas in a calculated and systematic way, I'd probably fall flat on my face. So I think it's better to fly by the seat of your pants.'

Boris Johnson, Tory MP

'Here in Devon we have to cope with people who come from as far afield as (cough) Somerset and even Wiltshire. I am having some difficulty living down the fact that I was born in Cornwall,'

Stanley Johnson, father of Boris, and Tory candidate for Teignbridge fielding reporters' questions regarding immigration

'They don't call me Tyrannosaurus Sex for nothing.'

Ted Kennedy, US Senator

— POLITICIANS ON THEMSELVES —

'I must keep up the suntan. It's a national institution after all.'

> *Robert Kilroy-Silk, former TV presenter and leader of Veritas*

'I'm a very keen ornithologist. Very interested in birds, and now I want to learn how to shoot them.'

> *Norman Lamont, former Chancellor of the Exchequer*

"If necessary, I would go out on the streets and beg rather than send them [his children] to the school next to where I live."

> *Oliver Letwin, Conservative MP*

'I am the nicest person I know and what I say is the truth as I see it.'

> *Peter Mandelson, former Labour MP and European Trade Commissioner*

"I have Bridget moments myself all the time"

> *Peter Mandelson speaks of his affection for Bridget Jones*

—POLITICIANS ON THEMSELVES—

'Nobody invites me out any more. I didn't think ahead. I didn't think that one day I would be a politician standing in my own right needing support, needing the political base that any politician requires.'

Peter Mandelson

'I've never been particularly bothered about my looks. No matter how I try, I've always been someone who looks a bit unkempt. It's just the way I am.'

Mo Mowlam, former Labour MP and former Northern Ireland Secretary

'I wanted to spend more time with my money.'
Steve Norris, former Conservative MP, explaining why he quit the Commons after 14 years

'I'm not thick-skinned; if anything, I'm too sensitive.'

John Prescott, Deputy Prime Minister

— POLITICIANS ON THEMSELVES —

'I always have a problem with my face: I have to live with it.'

John Prescott

'You can walk down the street and see who's working class and who's middle class. It's in the way we drive, the way we are, the way we dress. I am not getting back into whether I am middle class – clearly, I am,'

John Prescott

'I'm not smart enough to lie.'

Ronald Reagan, 40th US President

'I'm a terrible planner.'

Condoleezza Rice, US Secretary of State, responding to the questions of what she plans to do after the White House

'If I know the answer I'll tell you the answer, and, if I don't, I'll just respond, cleverly.'

Donald Rumsfeld, US Defence Secretary

—POLITICIANS ON THEMSELVES—

'I'm not indecisive. Am I indecisive?'
> *Jim Scheibel, former Mayor of St. Paul,*
> *Minnesota, now Director of Oxfam America*

'My relationship to power and authority is that
I'm all for it. People need somebody to watch
over them. Ninety-five per cent of the people in
the world need to be told what to do and how
to behave.'
> *Arnold Schwarzenegger, in a 1990*
> *interview with U.S. News*

'I was always dreaming about very powerful
people – dictators and things like that. I was just
always impressed by people who could be
remembered for hundreds of years, or even, like
Jesus, be for thousands of years remembered.'
> *Arnold Schwarzenegger, actor and Governor of*
> *California, in his 1977 film* Pumping Iron

'As you know, I don't need to take any money
from anybody. I have plenty of money myself. I
will make the decisions for the people.'
> *Arnold Schwarzenegger, speaking in 2003*

— POLITICIANS ON THEMSELVES —

'I have inhaled, exhaled everything.'
Arnold Schwarzenegger

"People have accused me of being in favour of globalisation. This is equivalent to accusing me of being in favour of the sun rising in the morning."
Clare Short, Labour MP

'I think I made a batch of buns once, but they came out deflated and saggy. I don't really think I qualify.'
Ann Widdecombe, Conservative MP, on being a domestic goddess

'I am passé. Tony Benn is passé. William Hague is passé. We are past our political prime but have lots to say.'
Ann Widdecombe

'No three-in-a-bed situations for me. Nor even two-in-a-bed. I don't do sex problems.'
Ann Widdecombe on her role as an agony aunt

—POLITICIANS ON THEMSELVES—

'I have sung it from the top deck of a cruise ship at 3am. I think of walking Dartmoor, looking round to make sure no one is listening to my tone-deaf notes, and singing from the top of every tor.'

Ann Widdecombe on her favourite hymn,
'How Great Thou Art'

'I was never one for bopping at parties.'

Ann Widdecombe

11

FAMOUS LAST WORDS

——— FAMOUS LAST WORDS ———

'I must have Irish blood myself. Every time
I speak in public I end up sounding like
James Joyce.'

George W. Bush, US President

'We've got hundreds of sites to exploit, looking
for the chemical and biological weapons that
we know Saddam Hussein had prior to our
entrance into Iraq.'

George W. Bush

'It'll be hard to articulate.'

*George W. Bush, on how he felt he would
feel on becoming US President*

'Politics gives guys so much power that they
tend to behave badly around women. I hope I
never get into that.'

Bill Clinton, 42nd US President

'I did not have sexual relations with
that woman.'

Bill Clinton, on Monica Lewinsky

——— FAMOUS LAST WORDS ———

'I don't have any real enemies'
> *Pim Fortuyn, former Dutch politician, soon*
> *before he was shot dead.*

"The whole nation loves him, because it feels safe in his hands, like a child in the arms of its mother.'
> *Joseph Goebbels, Nazi Propaganda Minister,*
> *on Adolf Hitler.*

'When Britain and the United States work together the world is a safer place.'
> *William Hague, former Conservative leader*

'I am savouring every single minute of the current exposure of the sanctimonious hypocrites and bare-faced liars who made so much political capital from so-called Tory sleaze in the last parliament.'
> *Neil Hamilton, disgraced former*
> *Conservative MP*

'We are winning international respect'
> *Adolf Hitler, German Nazi dictator*

——— FAMOUS LAST WORDS ———

'If the British attack our cities we will simply
erase theirs. The hour will come when one of us
will break up, and it won't be Nazi Germany.'

Adolf Hitler

'The wind will blow away foreign rattling as the
noise of an evil tyrant. You will never defeat me
this time. Never! Even if you come together
from all over the world and invite all the devils
as well, to stand by you.'

Saddam Hussein, former President
of Iraq, to the US government, marking the
34th anniversary of his Baath Party

'I have not the smallest molecule of faith in
aerial navigation other than ballooning.'

Lord Kelvin, 19th-century physicist and
President of the Royal Society

'I do not think we shall hear much more of the
general strike in our life'

Ramsay MacDonald, former British
Labour Prime Minister, in 1926

———— FAMOUS LAST WORDS ————

'Everyone in active politics has to be conscious of their sell-by date.'

> *Peter Mandelson, former Labour MP and*
> *European Trade Commissioner*

'I didn't mislead people. I know I didn't lie and I have got to establish that.'

> *Peter Mandelson*

'The truth is that men are tired of liberty.'

> *Benito Mussolini, Italian Fascist leader*

'I am not a crook.'

> *Richard Nixon, 37th US President*

'I'm glad I'm not Brezhnev. Being the Russian leader in the Kremlin. You never know if someone's tape recording what you say.'

> *Richard Nixon*

———— FAMOUS LAST WORDS ————

'Sure there are dishonest men in local government. But there are dishonest men in national government too.'

Richard Nixon

'I don't get a fair whack, I don't pursue vendettas or punch people on the nose.'

John Prescott, Deputy Prime Minister

'Public speaking is very easy.'

Dan Quayle, former US Prime Minister.
Other Dan Quayle quotes in this
book suggest otherwise

'I triple guarantee you. There are no American infidels in Baghdad.'

Mohammed Saeed al-Sahaf, (AKA 'Baghdad Bob'), former Iraqi Information Minister

'My feelings – as usual – we will slaughter them all.'

Mohammed Saeed al-Sahaf, on allied forces

———— FAMOUS LAST WORDS ————

'They are most welcome. We will butcher them.'
Mohammed Saeed al-Sahaf,
speaking about US troops:

'Faltering forces of infidels cannot just enter a
country of 26 million people and lay siege to
them! They are the ones who will find themselves under siege. Therefore, in reality whatever
this miserable Rumsfeld has been saying, he
was talking about his own forces. Now even the
American command is under siege.'
Mohammed Saeed al-Sahaf

'They're not even [within] 100 miles [of
Baghdad]. They are not in any place. They hold
no place in Iraq. This is an illusion ... they are
trying to sell to the others an illusion.'
Mohammed Saeed al-Sahaf

'They tried to bring a small number of tanks
and personnel carriers in through al-Durah but
they were surrounded and most of their infidels
had their throats cut.'
Mohammed Saeed al-Sahaf

———— FAMOUS LAST WORDS ————

'We're giving them a real lesson today. Heavy doesn't accurately describe the level of casualties we have inflicted.'

Mohammed Saeed al-Sahaf

'Iraqi fighters in Umm Qasr are giving the hordes of American and British mercenaries the taste of definite death. We have drawn them into a quagmire and they will never get out of it.'

Mohammed Saeed al-Sahaf

'Their infidels are committing suicide by the hundreds on the gates of Baghdad. Be assured, Baghdad is safe, protected.'

Mohammed Saeed al-Sahaf

'We defeated them yesterday. God willing, I will provide you with more information. I swear by God, I swear by God, those who are staying in Washington and London have thrown these mercenaries in a crematorium.'

Mohammed Saeed al-Sahaf

——— FAMOUS LAST WORDS ———

'God will roast their stomachs in hell at the hands of Iraqis.'

Mohammed Saeed al-Sahaf

'Nobody wants war. We do not want war. The United States, I am certain, does not want war.'

Jack Straw, Leader of the House

'It will be years, not in my time, before a woman will become Prime Minister.'

Margaret Thatcher, former British Prime Minister, in 1974

'You will be home before the leaves have fallen from the trees.'

Kaiser Wilhelm, Germany's last Kaiser, to German troops leaving for war in 1914

'Before man reaches the moon your mail will be delivered within hours from New York to Australia by guided missiles. We stand on the threshold of rocket mail.'

The US Postmaster General, speaking in 1959

———— FAMOUS LAST WORDS ————

'It is quite clear that the Tory Party will get rid of Mrs Thatcher in about three years' time.'
Sir Harold Wilson, former British Prime Minister, a year after The Iron Lady was elected. She won three more general elections after this

'I think all foreigners should stop interfering in the internal affairs of Iraq.'
Paul Wolfowitz, former US Deputy Defence Secretary

THE
POLITICIAN'S
WIFE (or husband)

THE POLITICIAN'S WIFE (or husband)

'He actually described his feelings in percentages, "I love you 60 per cent and her 40 per cent." Or the next day, "I love her 70 per cent and you 30 per cent." I alternated between feeling sorry for myself and sorry for him.'

> *Madeleine Albright, former US Secretary of State, on her husband's decision to leave her for a younger woman*

'Idi was a jolly person, very entertaining and kind. I think he was very kind to everyone.'

> *Sarah Amin, his fifth wife, on her husband*

'I don't know what normal is.'

> *Lady Archer, wife of disgraced Conservative peer, Jeffrey Archer*

'I think I should introduce him to my wife, because he is better-looking than [Massimo] Cacciari.'

> *Silvio Berlusconi, former Italian Prime Minister, on Danish Prime Minister Anders Fogh-Rasmussen. Mr Cacciari is a former Mayor of Venice rumoured to be romantically attached to Mrs Berlusconi*

THE POLITICIAN'S WIFE (or husband)

'I am always quite astonished when I read surveys about how many hours of housework men are supposed to do because in my experience they don't do any at all.'

Cherie Blair, QC and wife of Tony

'Aren't you getting a bit fat? Isn't it time you got back on your bike?'

Cherie Blair being frank with Tory MP Boris Johnson

'Once she goes to sleep it takes a minor nuclear explosion to wake her.'

Tony Blair, British Prime Minister, on his wife, Cherie

'You only require two things in life: your sanity and your wife.'

Tony Blair

"I've never sent her flowers. If I sent her flowers, she would get worried."

Tony Blair, on his wife, Cherie

THE POLITICIAN'S WIFE (or husband)

'What a media tragedy. She's like a fly trying to get out of a dollop of jam.'

>*Rory Bremner, comedian and impressionist, on Christine Hamilton*

'She usually goes on the bottom.'

>*James Carville, political consultant, responding to a New Hampshire voter who, talking about his marriage, asked, 'How do you do it?'*

Lady Astor: 'Winston, if I were your wife I'd put poison in your coffee.'
Winston Churchill: 'Nancy, if I were your husband I'd drink it.'

'I believe I'm a better authority than anybody else in America on my own wife. I have never known a person with a stronger sense of right and wrong in my life – ever.'

>*Bill Clinton, 42nd US President, on wife Hillary*

THE POLITICIAN'S WIFE (or husband)

'Staying married to my husband and running for the Senate are two of the very big choices I made. And I am grateful I made both of them.'

Hillary Clinton

'I think that, for both of us, this relationship has been the cornerstone of our lives. I find my husband the most alive, energised person ever and I feel so fortunate to have spent 30 years with him. I've learned and grown so much and I'm sure he'd say the same about me. So part of it is that you do sort of forgive what some might consider unforgivable.'

Hillary Clinton, on her relationship with Bill, in an interview with Good Housekeeping

'There was a time when those in public life attempted to behave with discretion and not like a stray mongrel in a public park.'

Lord Cobham, after his wife left him for David Mellor

THE POLITICIAN'S WIFE (or husband)

'He didn't read my memoirs. Like a lot of people, Robin doesn't really like keeping up with reality.'
Margaret Cook, former wife of Robin Cook, former Leader of the House of Commons

'For two, hard-working, committed people who care about each other to spend time in each other's company is nothing to be ashamed of.'
Edwina Currie, on her affair with John Major

'I am longing to iron a shirt again and get back to the normal things.'
Betsy Duncan Smith, having learned that her husband, Iain, had been officially cleared of misuse of parliamentary allowances

'She has a very big smile for a small woman.'
Germaine Greer, feminist writer and commentator, on Betsy Duncan Smith

'OK, I drink too much and Neil tells tasteless jokes, but that's our reality.'
Christine Hamilton, wife of former Conservative MP Neil Hamilton

THE POLITICIAN'S WIFE (or husband)

'Quite frankly, I don't want his nasty white suit anywhere near my red sofa.'
Christine Hamilton, refusing to interview Martin Bell on her TV programme

'I wouldn't change anything but I could do with sharing my bottom and thighs with at least two other people.'
Christine Hamilton, when asked which part of her body she would change

'To do as my mother tells me: drink less and stop taking my clothes off in public, even for charity.'
Christine Hamilton, on her New Year's resolution

'If I get up in the morning and there is a bottle of opened champagne in the fridge, then I am not averse to helping myself to a glass.'
Christine Hamilton

THE POLITICIAN'S WIFE (or husband)

'I'm a perfectly average woman. I'm not vain.
If I was, I wouldn't do it.'
> *Christine Hamilton, on her Botox treatment*

'We are like a pair of odd socks: I fit the right
foot, he fits the left.'
> *Christine Hamilton on her husband, Neil*

'By dragging his wife into the argument he was
not defending her honour, he was using her as
a sandbag.'
> *Lord Hattersley, Labour peer,*
> *on Iain Duncan Smith*

'He told me he had a confession to make. I
thought something saucy was going to come out.
But it was just that he couldn't put up shelves.'
> *Sandra Howard, on her husband, Michael,*
> *former Conservative leader*

'It's the tart that brings Michael out in broad
smiles,'
> *Sandra Howard on her husband Michael's*
> *infatuation for - treacle tart.*

THE POLITICIAN'S WIFE (or husband)

'He can't retire now. I'm not having him in
the house.'

> *Sandra Howard on her husband Michael*

'My husband cannot hide what he is feeling
because he is an honest animal.'

> *Sandra Howard*

'I have a soft spot for Cherie Blair.'

> *Boris Johnson, Tory MP, on his feelings for the
> Prime Minister's wife*

'Delia says, "Don't throw out all that leftover
wine. Freeze it into ice cubes for future use in
casseroles and sauce." Real women say, "What
leftover wine?"'

> *Glenys Kinnock, Labour MEP and wife
> of former Labour leader, Neil*

'I'm not happy about them moving here, but I
think the city's big enough for the two of us.'

> *Monica Lewinsky, on the Clintons
> relocating to New York City*

THE POLITICIAN'S WIFE (or husband)

'I'm a little leery when someone runs up and tells me what a big fan they are. Why are they fans? I have become an accidental celebrity. And, truly, it wasn't hard to do.'

Monica Lewinsky

'My wife's away. I have to dress myself.'
Denis MacShane, Labour MP, on why he was wearing 'extremely tacky House of Commons braces' at a book launch

'He is an extremely handsome man, with his humanity. He is a superior man, as a whole. He has strong feelings for other people, for their problems and needs. He is a good speaker, and he has inner stability, strong and natural, genetic inner stability.'
Mira Markovic, talking about her husband Slobodan Milosevic, former President of Yugoslavia

'In that place of evil, my husband fights for justice, facts, for everything that is good.'
Mira Markovic, on the UN War Crimes Court in The Hague where he faces a charge of genocide

THE POLITICIAN'S WIFE (or husband)

'Cherie Blair, I have a very hard relationship with. She has caused a lot of problems between Tony and the media. She is too aggressive. She bestows her patronage and then removes it on a whim. I said to Blair recently, "I would appreciate it if you stopped the missus trying to get me sacked."'

*Piers Morgan, former Editor of
the Daily Mirror*

"Wives shouldn't be there for terrorising,"
*John Prescott, Deputy Prime Minister, whose Hull
home was subject to a Greenpeace rooftop
protest when his wife Pauline was there*

'My wife has a very major cause and a very major interest that is a very complex and consuming issue with her. And that's me.'
Dan Quayle, former US Vice-President

'I'm just here for the drugs.'
*Nancy Reagan, wife of former US President
Ronald, at a 'Just Say No' event*

THE POLITICIAN'S WIFE (or husband)

'Yes, I do have a drinking problem: there's never enough.'

Denis Thatcher, husband of former British Prime Minister Margaret

'We have become a grandmother.'

Margaret Thatcher, former British Conservative Prime Minister. In view of this statement, Lord Prior commented, 'When Mrs Thatcher said, "We are a grandmother," she was including Denis in her remarks.'

'We have a BBC safety hazards form that we fill out before any production, but being kissed by Christine Hamilton didn't come into that unfortunately.'

Louis Theroux, TV presenter and documentary maker

13

BIZARRE POLITICAL SHITE

——BIZARRE POLITICAL SHITE——

'Hugging trees has a calming effect on me. I'm talking about enormous trees that will be there when we are all dead and gone. I've hugged trees in every part of this little island.'

Gerry Adams, President of Sinn Fein

'Fish and chips would be cheaper under Gore.'

Graham T. Allison, former co-chairman of Al Gore's foreign policy team, having been asked what difference a Gore or a Bush victory would make to Britain

'I am so clean you could eat your food off me.'

Tony Banks, former Labour MP

'People say, how can I help on this war against terror? How can I fight evil? You can do so by mentoring a child; by going into a shut-in's house and say I love you.'

George W. Bush, US President

—— BIZARRE POLITICAL SHITE ——

'President Musharraf, he's still tight with us on the war against terror, and that's what I appreciate. He's a – he understands that we've got to keep Al Qaeda on the run, and that, by keeping him on the run, it's more likely we will bring him to justice.'

George W. Bush

'I promise you I will listen to what has been said here, even though I wasn't here.'

George W. Bush

'There's nothing more deep than recognising Israel's right to exist. That's the most deep thought of all ... I can't think of anything more deep than that right.'

George W. Bush

'Sometimes when I sleep at night I think of [Dr. Seuss's] "Hop on Pop".'

George W. Bush

——— BIZARRE POLITICAL SHITE———

'It is time to set aside the old partisan bickering and finger-pointing and name-calling that comes from freeing parents to make different choices for their children.'

George W. Bush

'I mean, there needs to be a wholesale effort against racial profiling, which is illiterate children.'

George W. Bush

'I know the human being and fish can coexist peacefully.'

George W. Bush

'For me, pepper, I put it on my plate.'

Jean Chretien, former Canadian Prime Minister, commenting on the use of pepper spray by police at the World Trade Conference in Quebec City

—— BIZARRE POLITICAL SHITE ——

'I don't know what is marijuana. Perhaps I will try it when it will no longer be criminal. I will have my money for my fine and a joint in the other hand.'

Jean Chretien

'Now that we're on dog pee, we can have an interesting conversation about that. I do not recommend drinking urine ... but if you drink water straight from the river, you have a greater chance of getting an infection than you do if you drink urine.'

*Howard Dean, former US
Presidential candidate*

'Not only are we going to New Hampshire ... we're going to South Carolina and Oklahoma and Arizona and North Dakota and New Mexico, and we're going to California and Texas and New York! And we're going to South Dakota and Oregon and Washington and Michigan. And then we're going to Washington, D.C. to take back the White House, Yeeeeeaaaaaah!'

Howard Dean, in an Iowa concession speech

——— BIZARRE POLITICAL SHITE———

'Fishing is a passion. I often think that, when you are fishing, wildlife comes to you, because you are a peculiarity – a quiet human being.'

Iain Duncan Smith, former
Conservative leader

'If you don't mind smelling like peanut butter for two or three days, peanut butter is darn good shaving cream.'

Barry Goldwater, former US Senator

'Yes, I do talk to my trees. I did say to one, "You'd better smarten yourself up or you'll be gone" and the next year, well, you've never seen such a mass of flowers.'

Lord Michael Heseltine, Conservative peer

'I have information that the Government is planning to have me certified by psychiatrists.'

Ian Paisley, Northern Irish Politician

—— BIZARRE POLITICAL SHITE ——

'Having a pump is like having sex. I train two, sometimes three times a day. Each time I get a pump, it's great. I feel like I'm coming all day.'
Arnold Schwarzenegger, actor and Governor of California, on going down the gym

'The best activities for your health are pumping and humping.'
Arnold Schwarzenegger

'I am not quite certain what my right honourable friend said, but we hold precisely the same view.'
Margaret Thatcher, former British Conservative Prime Minister

'I especially love driving down a hill directly at a tree and swerving to one side at the last moment. That's my way to relax.'
Boris Yeltsin, former President of Russia

—BIZARRE POLITICAL BOLLOCKS—

'A government is not an old pair of socks that you throw out. Come to think of it, you don't throw out old pairs of socks anyway these days.'

Boris Yeltsin

14

ROYAL SHITE

———— ROYAL SHITE ————

'I have never drunk and never wanted to.
I can never understand how anyone can get
past the taste.'

Princess Anne, on alcohol

'The thing I might do best is be a long-distance
truck driver.'

Princess Anne

'We've never had a holiday. A week or two at
Balmoral, or ten days at Sandringham is the
nearest we get.'

Princess Anne

'Do you realise you are the first member of the
Royal Family to win an Oscar?'

*Anonymous US reporter, to Judi Dench,
who starred as Queen Elizabeth I*

'Prince Charles is so humble, and has this air
of old-fashioned charm and duty that is so
attractive.'

Lisa Barbuscia, model

——————— ROYAL SHITE ———————

'The Queen is not a fairy.'

*A Buckingham Palace spokesman, offering an
explanation of the large amount of medication
prescribed to Her Majesty*

'I like to tease George W. that the Prince of
Wales was much better dressed and
considerably more polite.'

Barbara Bush, on her son

'If these reports are true, as Prince Philip might
well have said, "it's none of his bloody
business".'

*Menzies Campbell, leader of the Liberal
Democrat, on reports that the Prince of Wales
had expressed concerns about the planned
European rapid reaction force*

'Sometimes as a bit of twit'

*Prince Charles, responding to David Frost's
enquiry as to how he would describe himself*

—————————— ROYAL SHITE ——————————

'If you have a sense of duty, and I like to think I have, service means that you give yourself to people, particularly if they want you, and sometimes if they don't.'

Prince Charles

'Awkward, cantankerous, cynical, bloody-minded, at times intrusive, at times inaccurate and at times deeply unfair and harmful to individuals and to institutions.'

Prince Charles, on the press

'If I hear one more joke about being hit in the face with a carnation by a Bolshevik fascist lady, I don't know what I'll do.'

Prince Charles, referring to an incident in Latvia when a 16-year-old schoolgirl slapped him in the face with a bunch of carnations. 'I'm very glad it's given pleasure to everybody,' he added. 'It's what I'm here for.'

'If I'm deciding on whom I want to live with for 50 years, well that's the last decision on which I would want my head to be ruled by my heart.'

Prince Charles, speaking in 1972

──────── ROYAL SHITE ────────

'Dig that crazy rhythm.'
> *Prince Charles, trying to get down with*
> *the kids at a Prince's Trust shelter*

'It's like swimming in undiluted sewage'
> *Prince Charles, emerging from the*
> *sea in Melbourne. His remarks didn't earn him*
> *any brownie points with the Australians,*
> *and the press went mad.*

'I expect a thirty-year apprenticeship before
I am king.'
> *Prince Charles*

'I now complete the process of helping my
father to expose himself.'
> *Prince Charles, unveiling a sculpture*
> *of Prince Philip*

'Who is Llewellyn?'
> *Prince Charles, questioning the name on a*
> *banner at his investiture in Wales. Llewellyn was*
> *the previous Prince of Wales.*

ROYAL SHITE

'I want to make certain that I have some plants left to talk to.'

> *Prince Charles, opening the*
> *Millennium Seed Bank*

'These bloody people. I can't bear that man. He is so awful, he really is.'

> *Prince Charles on royal correspondent*
> *Nicholas Witchell*

'It's a thousand years of breeding'

> *Prince Charles, when asked in New York how he*
> *can act 'charming and not look tired and bored*
> *at everyone's questions'*

'She wore such awful shift dresses. I wouldn't say she was someone with innate style.'

> *Susannah Constantine, TV style guru,*
> *on Princess Diana*

'Oh, I'm so sorry, I didn't recognise you without your crown.'

> *Lady Diana Cooper, realising at a party that the*
> *woman she was talking to was Queen Elizabeth II*

———— ROYAL SHITE ————

'We were bunk buddies. I have to say it made me the republican I am today.'

Andrew Day, Prince Andrew's Gordonstoun
room-mate, on the monarchy

'I think the biggest disease the world suffers from in this day and age is the disease of people feeling unloved. I know that I can give love for a minute, for half an hour, for a day, for a month, but I can give. I am very happy to do that. I want to do that.'

Diana, Princess of Wales

'A Leper Colony.'

Princess Diana, on the Royal Family

'Well, naturally it is quite daunting, but I hope it won't be too difficult, and with Prince Charles beside me I can't go wrong.'

Lady Diana Spencer, speaking in 1981

—————————— ROYAL SHITE ——————————

'Life is a journey that does not end once you find happiness or your true self and I want to let people know I have the same struggles as them.'
Sarah Ferguson, the Duchess of York,
referring to her autobiography

'Most people call their dogs Fergie. I'm kind of proud. You hear it in the park, "Fergie, come here."'
Sarah Ferguson, on dogs

'I'm doing pretty well considering. You know, in the past, when anyone left the Royal Family they had you beheaded.'
Sarah Ferguson

'I couldn't believe it the other day when I picked up a British newspaper and read that 82 per cent of men would rather sleep with a goat than me.'
Sarah Ferguson

——————— ROYAL SHITE ———————

'Make a friend of your mind. Free your mind, and your bottom will follow.'
Sarah Ferguson, giving slimming advice

"I'm single. I'm skinny. I still can't find a man."
Sarah Ferguson

'When she was nice she was very, very nice. Some of the time she was horrid.'
Patrick Jephson, former royal servant, defending his book on Princess Diana

'It was all right. I shook hands and it was quite nice. I'm a big fan of the royals but there's a lot more other people I'd rather meet.'
Vinnie Jones, ex-footballer turned actor, on meeting the Queen

'The Queen doesn't like music. She always looks so bloody bored. I only play for her if she pays me.'
Nigel Kennedy, violinist

——————— ROYAL SHITE ———————

'Camilla's an attractive bird, isn't she? She's got a nice figure and nice legs. She's strangely attractive, like Mrs Simpson.'

Spike Milligan, comedian, on
Camilla Parker-Bowles

'I was in Swaziland where the centre of attention was the King's selection of a tenth wife. If only our royal family were as conventional.'

Matthew Parris, political commentator and
former Conservative MP

'You were playing your instruments, weren't you? Or do you have tape recorders under your seats?'

Prince Philip, 'congratulating' a school band on
their performance in Australia, in 2002

'Just as we can't blame people for their parents, we can't blame South America for not having been members of the British Empire.'

Prince Philip, at the British and
Latin Chambers of Commerce

——————— ROYAL SHITE ———————

'Reichskanzler.'
Prince Philip's welcome greeting to German leader Helmut Kohl. Hitler was the most recent chancellor to use the title.

'A few years ago everybody was saying, "We must have more leisure, everybody's working too much." Now that everybody's got more leisure, they're complaining they're unemployed. They don't seem to be able to make up their minds what they want, do they?'
Prince Philip, on the recession

'I rather doubt whether anyone has ever been genuinely shocked by anything I have said.'
Prince Philip

'What a po-faced lot these Dutch are.'
Prince Philip, on a visit to Holland

———— ROYAL SHITE ————

'I talk too much about things of which I have never claimed any special knowledge, just contemplate the horrifying prospect if I were to get my teeth into something even remotely familiar.'

Prince Philip

'You can't have been here that long, you haven't got a potbelly.'

Prince Philip, to a Briton residing in Hungary

'If a cricketer, for instance, suddenly decided to go into a school and batter a lot of people to death with a cricket bat, which he could do very easily, are you going to ban cricket bats?'

Prince Philip, responding to calls to ban firearms after the Dunblane massacre

'Are you Indian or Pakistani? I can never tell the difference between you chaps.'

Prince Philip, at a Washington Embassy reception for Commonwealth members

—————— ROYAL SHITE ——————

'If it has got four legs and it is not a chair, if it has two wings and it flies but is not an aeroplane, and if it swims and it is not a submarine, the Cantonese will eat it.'
Prince Philip, commenting on Chinese eating habits to a WWF conference in 1986

'Ghastly'
Prince Philip, on Beijing, China, in 1986

'Are you still throwing spears at other tribes?'
Prince Philip, to an Aborigine elder, on a royal visit to Australia.

'It's too bad you sent your royal family to the guillotine, isn't it?'
Prince Philip, to a French minister

'The monarchy exists not for its own benefit, but for that of the country. If you don't want us, then let's end it on amicable terms and not have a row about it. We don't come here for our health. We can think of better ways of enjoying ourselves.'
Prince Philip, visiting Canada

─────────── ## ROYAL SHITE ───────────

'It looks as if it was put in by an Indian.'
Prince Philip, pointing at an old-fashioned
fuse box while on a tour of a factory near
Edinburgh in 1993

'I declare this thing open – whatever it is.'
Prince Philip, at the opening of Vancouver City
Hall's new Annexe

'Deaf? If you are near there, no wonder you
are deaf.'
Prince Philip, to deaf people, in reference to a
nearby school's steel band, playing in his honour

'I think it is a perfectly valid system for
producing a head of state. It's been very
successful for 1,000 years. It's had its ups and
downs, undoubtedly.'
Prince Philip, on the monarchy

'The problem with London is the tourists.
They cause the congestion. If we could just stop
tourism then we could stop the congestion.'
Prince Philip, on London's
congestion charge

—————— ROYAL SHITE ——————

'Aren't most of you descended from pirates?'
*Prince Philip, to a wealthy resident
of the Cayman Islands*

'I never see any home cooking – all I get is
fancy stuff'
Prince Philip

It's a pleasant change to be in a country that
isn't ruled by its people.
*Prince Philip, to Alfredo Stroessner, the
Paraguayan dictator*

'I have never been to Burma and I have never
even seen the place. I cannot say I am very
sorry. I am not particularly fond of rain.'
*Prince Philip, at the Burma Star
Association Reunion*

'How do you keep the natives off the booze
long enough to get them to pass the test?'
*Prince Philip quizzes a Scottish
driving instructor*

─────── ROYAL SHITE ───────

'You managed not to get eaten then.'
Prince Philip to a student who had just visited
Papua New Guinea

'Dontopedalogy is the science of opening your
mouth and putting you foot in it, a science
which I have practised for a good many years.'
Prince Philip

'If you gave a seven-year-old a brush and some
paints he'd produce something like that.'
Prince Philip, on viewing paintings in
Sudan's national museum

'So you're responsible for the kind of crap
Channel Four produces'
Prince Philip, to the chairman
of Channel Four

──────── ROYAL SHITE ────────

'If you travel as much as we do, you appreciate how much more comfortable aircraft have become. Unless you travel in something called economy class, which sounds ghastly.'

Prince Philip, during the Royal Jubilee tour in 2002

'You shouldn't stay here too long or you'll turn slitty eyed.'

Prince Philip, talking to British students in China

'The best thing to do with a degree is forget it.'

Prince Philip

'No, I might catch some ghastly disease.'

Prince Philip, on being offered to stroke a koala bear.

'The point is that young people are the same as they always were: they are just as ignorant.'

Prince Philip

——————— ROYAL SHITE ———————

'You never know, it could be somebody important.'

Queen Elizabeth II, advising an embarrassed young woman to answer her mobile phone which rang while they were in conversation

'Manchester, that's not such a nice place.'

Queen Elizabeth II

'Unless one is there, it's embarrassing. Like hearing the Lord's Prayer while playing canasta.'

The Queen Mother, speaking of the National Anthem

'We'd be a drearier and somehow bleaker place. We'd end up needing some sort of tribal, symbolic, emblematic figure to personify us and I just don't know if David Beckham's ready for the job ... yet.'

Simon Schama, historian, on what would happen if the monarchy were dissolved

ROYAL SHITE

'I met Princess Anne and said, "I like your hair."
It was tongue in cheek because I hate her hair,
but she thought it was for real and said, "Oh, I
do the front and my hairdresser does the back."'
*Trevor Sorbie, after being appointed
hairdresser to the Queen*

'There she is, the huge vast bulk of her.'
*Wynford Vaughan-Thomas. The BBC's man made
the comment as the camera switched to a view of
the Queen Mum at a launch of the Ark Royal*

'The Queen thought it was hilarious. I met one
of her courtiers and he told me she still giggles
about the day Vivienne came to get her medal.'
*Vivienne Westwood, fashion designer, on the
time she forgot to wear her knickers when she
went to collect her OBE*

'The little buggers nip.'
*William Whitelaw, former Conservative
MP, warning former Conservative Chancellor
Kenneth Clarke about the Queen's corgis*

——— ACKNOWLEDGEMENTS ———

A huge thank-you to all of the friends and family who sent us so many quotes. We never expected such a helpful response and couldn't have done this without you. You know who you are.

Also, our heartfelt thanks go to all of the anonymous individuals who bothered to note these gems of speech down in the first place, and to the innumerable websites that provided us with so many fantastic quotes. Without you, this and other anthologies would not exist. Also, the biggest thanks of all goes to George W. Bush and his administration, and Mohammed Saeed al-Sahaf. We may not have found any Weapons of Mass Destruction, but boy did we find comedians in you!